FEB 1 6 2012

D0946481

Issues in the Digital Age

Online Gaming and Entertainment

Other titles in the series include:

Online Communication and Social Networking
Online Information and Research
Online Predators
Online Privacy
Online Security

Issues in the Digital Age

Online Gaming and Entertainment

Hal Marcovitz

ReferencePoint
Press®

San Diego, CA

© 2012 ReferencePoint Press, Inc.
Printed in the United States

For more information, contact:
ReferencePoint Press, Inc.
PO Box 27779
San Diego, CA 92198
www. ReferencePointPress.com

ALL RIGHTS RESERVED.
No part of this work covered by the copyright hereon may be reproduced or used in any form or by any means—graphic, electronic, or mechanical, including photocopying, recording, taping, web distribution, or information storage retrieval systems—without the written permission of the publisher.

LIBRARY OF CONGRESS CATALOGING-IN-PUBLICATION DATA

Marcovitz, Hal.
  Online gaming and entertainment / by Hal Marcovitz.
    p. cm. — (Issues in the digital age)
  Includes bibliographical references and index.
  ISBN-13: 978-1-60152-191-0 (hardback)
  ISBN-10: 1-60152-191-X (hardback)
  1. Internet games—Juvenile literature. 2. Computer games—Juvenile literature. I. Title.
  GV1469.15.M37 2012
  794.8—dc23

                                                            2011018701

Contents

3 0053
00983
0319

A Vast Source of Entertainment

Vishal Singh, a senior at Woodside High School in Redwood City, California, hopes to major in filmmaking in college. In fact, he is already an accomplished filmmaker, having posted several of the short movies he has produced on the online site Vimeo. And Singh has also established his own website where friends and fans can view his films.

He typically spends many hours online each week, watching movies made by other student filmmakers on Vimeo as well as YouTube and other online video sites. Singh is also something of a video game fan and admits to spending at least 10 hours a week playing games.

As for schoolwork, though, Singh has had some bumpy times. Entering his senior year at Woodside, he was carrying a D average after flunking algebra. Moreover, with just a few weeks to go before the start of the fall semester, he had barely cracked open the book assigned for his summer reading project, *Cat's Cradle* by novelist Kurt Vonnegut. Instead of reading the book, Singh preferred to find information about the novel posted on YouTube and other websites. "You can get a whole story [on it] in six minutes," says Singh. "A book takes so long. I prefer the immediate gratification."[1]

Many Opportunities for Entertainment

Singh's story illustrates the two sides of Internet-based entertainment. On the one hand, the Internet has provided young people like Singh and others with vast resources to find entertainment while also exploring their own creative abilities. Indeed, by the spring of 2011 Singh had posted nearly 20 of his short films on Vimeo. They included titles such as *Compromise*, a 30-second comedy showing Singh fistfighting himself in the style reminiscent of the era of silent movies, and *L'Ecole*, in which an introspective French exchange student walks the lonely halls of a high school, reflecting on her experiences in America. Singh's films display skillful production techniques, including brisk editing as well as the use of background music and narration.

For other Internet users who just like to watch videos or listen to music or play games, there is no shortage of opportunities to find many entertaining activities online. According to a 2010 study by the Washington, DC–based Pew Internet & American Life Project, 83 percent of American Internet users pursue their hobbies online; 72 percent go online just for fun, 66 percent watch videos online, 37 percent download music, and 35 percent play online games. "Listening to music and watching online videos are among the most common of the activities we evaluated; roughly half of all online . . . users have done each of these activities to relax," says the Pew analysis. "Young Americans in particular go online in great numbers to relax by watching videos, listening to music, playing games or chatting with friends."[2]

> "Listening to music and watching online videos are among the most common of the activities we evaluated; roughly half of all online . . . users have done each of these activities to relax."[2]
>
> — Pew Internet & American Life Project.

Too Much Time Online

However, the vast amount of entertainment available on the Internet can also dominate the lives of Internet users—which illustrates the other side of Singh's story. In Singh's case his devotion to the Internet has affected his grades. Marcia Blondel, an English teacher at Woodside High School, says Singh is one of many students who find it difficult to pull themselves away from the entertainment they find on the Internet long enough to concentrate on their studies. "You can't become a good writer while watching YouTube,"[3] she says.

For many young people and others, poor performance in school or on the job may be the least of the dangers found in spending too much time enjoying the entertainment they find on the Internet. Many forms

Online Activities by Age

Percent of Internet users in each generation who engage in this online activity

| | 0–9% | | 10–19% | | 20–29% | | 30–39% | | 40–49% |
| | 50–59% | | 60–69% | | 70–79% | | 80–89% | | 90–100% |

Ages 18–33	Ages 34–45	Ages 46–55	Ages 56–64	Ages 65–73	Ages 74+
E-mail	E-mail	E-mail	E-mail	E-mail	E-mail
Search	Search	Search	Search	Search	Search
Health info	Health info	Health info	Health info	Health info	Health info
Social network sites	Get news	Get news	Get news	Get news	Buy a product
Watch video	Gov't website	Gov't website	Gov't website	Travel reservations	Get news
Get news	Travel reservations	Travel reservations	Buy a product	Buy a product	Travel reservations
Buy a product	Watch video	Buy a product	Travel reservations	Gov't website	Gov't website
IM	Buy a product	Watch video	Bank online	Watch video	Bank online
Listen to music	Social network sites	Bank online	Watch video	Financial info	Financial info
Travel reservations	Bank online	Social network sites	Social network sites	Bank online	Religious info
Online classifieds	Online classifieds	Online classifieds	Online classifieds	Rate things	Watch video
Bank online	Listen to music	Listen to music	Financial info	Social network sites	Play games
Gov't website	IM	Financial info	Rate things	Online classifieds	Online classifieds
Play games	Play games	IM	Listen to music	IM	Social network sites
Read blogs	Financial info	Religious info	Religious info	Religious info	Rate things
Financial info	Religious info	Rate things	IM	Play games	Read blogs
Rate things	Read blogs	Read blogs	Play games	lISten to music	Donate to charity
Religious info	Rate things	Play games	Read blogs	Read blogs	Listen to music
Online auction	Online auction	Online auction	Online auction	Donate to charity	Podcasts
Podcasts	Donate to charity	Donate to charity	Donate to charity	Online auction	Online auction
Donate to charity	Podcasts	Podcasts	Podcasts	Podcasts	Blog
Blog	Blog	Blog	Blog	Blog	IM
Virtual worlds	Virtual worlds	Virtual worlds	Virtual worlds	Virtual worlds	Virtual worlds

Source: Pew Internet & American Life Project, "Generations 2010: What Different Generations Do Online," December 16, 2010. www.pewinternet.org.

of Internet entertainment—particularly gaming and gambling—can draw users in so deeply that they develop addictions to those activities.

Meanwhile, many people will knowingly watch pirated versions of movies online—meaning the films are available for viewing over the Internet without permission of the studios that produce them. People who watch pirated films online deprive the copyright owners of the fees or royalties they would otherwise earn if the viewers bought tickets to see the movies in the theaters or purchased or rented the films on DVD.

That is also true of music, which is widely available online and also widely stolen, denying the composers, recording artists, and other professionals the royalties that should be rightfully theirs. Says a statement by the Recording Industry Association of America (RIAA), the trade organization that represents music professionals:

> "You can't become a good writer while watching YouTube."[3]
>
> —Marcia Blondel, English teacher, Woodside High School.

It's commonly known as "piracy," but that's too benign of a term to adequately describe the toll that music theft takes on the enormous cast of industry players working behind the scenes to bring music to your ears. That cast includes songwriters, recording artists, audio engineers, computer technicians, talent scouts and marketing specialists, producers, publishers and countless others. While downloading one song may not feel that serious of a crime, the accumulative impact of millions of songs downloaded illegally—and without any compensation to all the people who helped to create that song and bring it to fans—is devastating.[4]

The RIAA has sponsored a poll indicating that 70 percent of Internet users know it is illegal to download pirated music—yet they do it anyway. It is also likely that many online video fans like Singh know it is probably not in their best interest to spend so much time online—and yet they also acknowledge just how hard it is to pull themselves away.

Chapter One

How the Internet Dominates the Entertainment World

The world of Internet entertainment changed dramatically on April 23, 2005. That is the day a brief video of Jawed Karim visiting the San Diego Zoo was posted online. The video was titled simply *Me at the Zoo* and featured 18 seconds of Karim standing in front of a group of elephants.

Despite its lack of action, plot, or enticing dialogue, *Me at the Zoo* made Internet history. It was the first video uploaded onto the website known as YouTube. The site had been created by Karim and two friends, Chad Hurley and Steve Chen, who had discovered, several months before, the difficulties of sharing videos online. The three men, all coworkers, had attended a dinner party together where they shot brief videos of the guests. Later, when they tried to exchange the videos online, they discovered the lack of software to easily accomplish the task.

So they wondered whether a website could be developed that would make it easier to share video files, and they also wondered whether there were many people, like themselves, who would appreciate the entertainment value of online video. "It was pretty simple," says Hurley. "We removed the barriers for people to upload videos."[5]

Going Viral

YouTube would, in fact, prove to be highly successful. Just six months after *Me at the Zoo* aired on YouTube, tens of thousands of other videos had been posted on the website. Moreover, the site was receiving some 700 million views a week. People were not only posting videos shot by amateurs but also professionally produced footage digitally recorded from TV broadcasts. When a YouTube fan uploaded a digitized version of a brief *Saturday Night Live* film titled *Lazy Sunday*—a hip-hop story about a couple of nerdy stoners—it went viral, recording some 5 million views within a matter of days.

One of the featured players in the film, comedian Andy Samberg, was just beginning his career on *Saturday Night Live*. Samberg believes the availability of the film on YouTube helped boost his career. "I've been recognized more times since the Saturday it aired [on YouTube] than

The video-sharing website YouTube logs approximately 20 million individual visitors per month. Since its debut in 2005, viewers have posted more than 2.5 billion videos on the site.

The 10 Billionth Download

According to the Nielsen Company, which charts the popularity of entertainment media, record companies sold 428 million albums on CDs in 2009. While that may appear to be an impressive number, the statistic signals that sales of CDs are on the decline. Two years earlier, Nielsen reported, record companies had sold more than 500 million CDs.

CDs are losing market share to music sold over the Internet in the MP3 format. In 2010 iTunes—the largest MP3 sales company—announced that it had sold its 10 billionth download. And when iTunes revealed the identity of the buyer, the news illustrated that MP3 files are not just a technology favored by young fans of the Black Eyed Peas or Lady Gaga. The music fan who downloaded the 10 billionth song was 71-year-old Louie Sulcer of Woodstock, Georgia, who bought a download of the late country singer Johnny Cash's 1958 hit "Guess Things Happen That Way."

iTunes is owned by computer maker Apple. Shortly after Sulcer downloaded the song, he received a call from Apple chair Steve Jobs, who informed Sulcer he had won $10,000 in free downloads. Jobs also arranged for Sulcer to chat with Johnny Cash's daughter Roseanne, who told Sulcer, "We're so proud that the winning pick was one of my dad's songs."

Quoted in CBS News, "Apple Marks 10 Billionth Song Download," February 26, 2010. www.cbsnews.com.

since I started the show," Samberg said shortly after the film was posted online. "It definitely felt like something changed overnight."[6]

Today YouTube is one of the most popular sites on the World Wide Web. Fans post more than 65,000 new videos a day on the site. Overall, viewers have posted more than 2.5 billion videos on YouTube that are watched by some 20 million individual visitors per month. That staggering volume of traffic illustrates the enormous capability of the Internet to serve as an entertainment source.

Catching Up on *Gossip Girl*

YouTube is not the sole source of online video, although it is believed that the website does account for 60 percent of the videos available on the Internet. Still, there are other sources. The TV networks NBC, ABC, and Fox have collaborated on Hulu, a website where viewers can find complete shows from those networks as well as excerpts, promos, and behind-the-scenes footage. By 2009 some 9 million viewers per day were watching shows such as *Fringe* and *30 Rock* on Hulu rather than on the TV sets in their living rooms.

Such TV fare is available elsewhere on the Internet as well. All the major broadcast TV networks as well as the cable networks have now made their most popular shows available on their own websites. A loyal follower of *Gossip Girl* who missed the previous week's episode can find it on the website of the CW Television Network. Fans of *Real World* who miss an occasional episode can catch up with the tribulations of the cast members on MTV's website. Stephen Colbert's fans can keep up with his gags on Comedy Central's website. In 2010 a study by the Pew Internet & American Life Project reported that 69 percent of Internet users watch videos online. The percentage is even higher among young people: Pew reported that as many as 89 percent of teenagers and young children watch videos online.

Meanwhile, about 14 percent of Internet users regularly upload videos onto the Internet. Says Mary Madden, a senior research specialist for Pew: "Young adults are among the most contagious carriers when it comes to understanding how viral videos propagate online. Younger users are the most eager and active contributors to the online video sphere; they are more likely than older users to watch, upload, rate, comment upon and share the video they find."[7]

> "Younger users are the most eager and active contributors to the online video sphere; they are more likely than older users to watch, upload, rate, comment upon and share the video they find."[7]
>
> —Mary Madden, senior research specialist for the Pew Internet & American Life Project.

Limited Capabilities of Computers

While watching videos on the Internet is now a routine pastime enjoyed by tens of millions of people a day, that has not always been the case. Throughout much of the history of the Internet, it was impossible for most people to watch even the briefest of videos. Computers had limited ability to process information, and Internet service providers had limited ability to deliver large quantities of information over telephone lines. Technological advances over a relatively short period of time made it possible to overcome these obstacles.

The Internet was born on October 29, 1969, when computers at the University of California at Los Angeles and Stanford University in Palo Alto, California, communicated with one another, transmitting a very brief text message over a distance of about 300 miles (483km). The Internet was conceived as a way for military computers to share information in the event normal modes of communication were shut down due to warfare. By the late 1970s, though, the Internet had been opened to civilian use. Most users were computer engineers who shared information over what was known as Usenet—essentially an online bulletin board created by graduate students at Duke University in North Carolina.

> "The vision of the Internet as a multimedia servant that offers you a host of audio and video delights is not merely fantasy, it's fraud. It will be years before the Internet can begin to compete with MTV or HBO."[8]
>
> —*Popular Science* magazine in 1995.

During the 1980s, consumer access to the Internet exploded as early Internet service providers such as America Online (now known as AOL), Prodigy, Genie, and CompuServe sold memberships to subscribers who typically paid $10 or $20 a month to connect to the providers' home pages. The home computers of the era—and the microprocessors that enabled them to deliver information on their screens—were far less powerful than what is typically found today. This was the era of the Apple II, Commodore 64, and IBM PC—computers that could be used to draft letters or do homework, play rudimentary games, and display simple graphics. They were very popular among consumers, but when compared with today's sophisticated laptops, desktops, smartphones, and tablets, their capabilities were rather limited.

Moreover, to connect to America Online or the other Internet providers, computers employed what was known as dial-up service. The modems were connected to the phone lines in the subscribers' homes—they actually dialed the phone numbers for the Internet service providers, making audible clicking sounds as they connected. (Even today, mostly in rural communities where so-called broadband service is unavailable, many Internet users still rely on dial-up providers to connect to the Internet.)

The Internet Expands

Dial-up service was notoriously slow, and along with the slow speed of the microprocessors, it was tediously difficult to watch videos online. America Online and the other providers tried to spruce up their home pages with photos and other graphics as well as the occasional brief video, but it would take several minutes for the computer to process all the information it would need to display a video that might last no more than a few seconds. Few subscribers had the patience to sit in front of a screen that was frozen while the central processing unit untangled all the information required to run the video clips.

As computer engineers worked to resolve the problems of slow download speeds and slow microprocessors, it was clear the Internet was expanding, providing people with more places to find information—including entertainment. In 1991 Swiss computer engineer Tim Berners-Lee developed the concept of the uniform resource locator, or URL, which led to the establishment of the World Wide Web. Early Internet browsers such as Mosaic and Internet Explorer enabled users to jump from website to website. In 1993 there were just 130 nontechnical websites available on the World Wide Web; by 2009 there were 130 million.

Even with these advances, it still took a long time for computers to make the connections and display the information on their screens. If a computer user found an interesting video online, watching it still required tremendous patience. In 1995 the magazine *Popular Science* predicted that the Internet would not be capable of providing watchable video entertainment for many years:

> The Web is s-l-o-w. Often excruciatingly slow. That's because the Web is transporting graphics-laden documents, not just plain text, and there's not much room in the phone company's copper wires for visuals. The more pictures in the document, the longer it takes to appear on your PC screen. Even with a fast modem, waiting ten to 20 seconds for a single page is typical. Waitin minute or more is not unusual. . . .

Receiving a digitized audio or video clip can require the patience of Job. Short clips can take 15 minutes; longer ones can take a half hour or more. Even then, the quality of the pictures and sounds is considerably inferior to your TV and CD player. . . . The vision of the Internet as a multimedia servant that offers you a host of audio and video delights is not merely fantasy, it's fraud. It will be years before the Internet can begin to compete with MTV or HBO.[8]

As things turned out, it would take a lot less time for the Internet to become a viable medium for video and other entertainment than *Popular Science* had predicted. By the early years of the twenty-first century, telecommunications companies had modernized their phone lines and wireless networks, making them capable of transmitting huge amounts of data. Fiber-optic cables replaced copper telephone wires. Cable TV providers found they could carry Internet signals through their cables as well. The computers improved as engineers developed very powerful microprocessors. Now, computers sold to consumers are capable of carrying video images in "real time," making the computer an integral component of home entertainment.

Online Gaming Evolves Slowly

Even in the era when the briefest of videos would take thirty minutes or more to download, game players could find plenty of diversions online. Indeed, the history of online gaming dates back to the earliest days of the Internet. In the early 1970s, when the Internet was still in its infancy, it was used predominantly by computer engineers to share data. But engineers also enjoyed playing games, and many of the early Internet users could go online to play a rudimentary game known as *Spacewar!* Essentially, *Spacewar!* enabled the players—pilots of opposing spaceships—to fire missiles at one another. Each spaceship was represented on the screen as a blip of light. The missiles were smaller blips of light.

Avid gamers who enjoyed maneuvering a frog through a maze or helping a plucky little hero named Mario jump over barrels in his quest to save a princess from a big ape did not find their favorite games available on the Internet but, rather, on game cartridges that were inserted

Playing *Colossal Cave Adventure*

"You are standing at the end of a road before a small brick building. Around you is a forest. A small stream flows out of the building and down a gully. . . ."

That is how players of *Colossal Cave Adventure* began their journeys. Today, in a typical game, players would actually see graphic representations of the brick building, forest, stream, and gully on their screens, but when the game was introduced in 1975, players had to make do with text descriptions of the game environment.

It took a lot of imagination for *Colossal Cave Adventure* players to picture themselves groping their way through the dark recesses of Mammoth Cave. Not only was the cave described in text form, but players had to respond to the challenges in text. Before beginning, players were advised to read this tutorial:

> Somewhere nearby is Colossal Cave, where others have found fortunes in treasure and gold, though it is rumored that some who enter are never seen again. Magic is said to work in the cave. I will be your eyes and hands. Direct me with commands of 1 or 2 words. I should warn you that I look at only the first five letters of each word, so you'll have to enter "northeast" as "ne" to distinguish it from "north." (Should you get stuck, type "help" for some general hints. For information on how to end your adventure, etc., type "info.")

Quoted in Dennis G. Jerz, "Colossal Cave Adventure," *Jerz's Literacy Weblog*, September 10, 2010. http://jerz.setonhill.edu.

into dedicated consoles made by Atari, Coleco, Nintendo, and other manufacturers. By the early 1980s many popular games were also produced on floppy disks so they could be played on computers, but they still were not available on the Internet.

Online game playing evolved slowly—mostly because of the same constraints that held back the availability of online videos. However, in 1975 game players were provided with a glimpse of the future when computer programmer Will Crowther developed a rudimentary game for the Internet titled *Colossal Cave Adventure*. Crowther enjoyed exploring caves, particularly Mammoth Cave in Kentucky, which features spectacularly colorful caverns, dramatic rock formations, underground streams, and towering rock chimneys. He devised a game for his daughters to play that would enable them to explore a virtual version of a cave. He also made it available to everyone for free on the Internet.

Exploring a Cave—in Text

People who play video games today would hardly recognize *Colossal Cave Adventure* as a game. The cave was described in text, posing challenges to the cave explorers. Players responded by typing commands in text, such as "GO NORTH" or "GET TORCH." Says Matt Barton, a college English professor and an authority on Internet gaming, "Although primitive even by the standards of later text-based adventure games, *Colossal Cave Adventure* established a new gaming paradigm."[9]

> **"Although primitive even by the standards of later text-based adventure games, *Colossal Cave Adventure* established a new gaming paradigm."[9]**
>
> —Matt Barton, college English professor and authority on Internet gaming.

As with most Internet-based games, the play was limited mostly to people who had access to the Internet—for the most part, other computer engineers. Still, *Colossal Cave Adventure* proved to be enormously popular and attracted a wide audience among Internet users of the era. One of the game's fans was Stanford University graduate student Don Woods, who expanded the concept—introducing fantasy elements into the experience. *Colossal Cave Adventure* players still had to negotiate their way through a text-based game, but now they would be faced with much different obstacles to overcome than just a pitch-black cavern. For instance, a text-based dragon might be lurking in their path. Says Barton, "Woods pushed the game . . . further towards what would eventually become the adventure game as we know it today."[10]

State-of-the-Art Graphics

As computers were equipped with more powerful microprocessors and as the Internet became more accessible to consumers and better able to carry large amounts of data, game playing moved beyond the text versions of *Colossal Cave Adventure* and similar games. In 1980 Internet users could play the first online game employing graphics, *Mystery House*.

The game required players to find their way through an abandoned Victorian mansion, featuring all manner of hidden dangers. *Mystery House* made use of crude line drawings, but nevertheless it was far more advanced than the texting experience of *Colossal Cave Adventure*. Three years after *Mystery House* made its debut on the Internet, players found the action far more enticing in the *King's Quest* series of games. In the *King's Quest* series, players entered mythological kingdoms where they were called on to assume the roles of sword-wielding heroes, face evil creatures, traipse through moats, and overcome all manner of other obstacles.

Gamers who like to interact with other players and match wits with adversaries are drawn to multiplayer online games. Multiplayer online gaming is a worldwide phenomenon, as can be seen in this photograph of a college student in China who is playing World of Warcraft.

From those humble beginnings, the online gaming experience exploded in the 1990s as computers and their microprocessors became even more powerful while bandwidth—the ability to deliver content over the Internet—expanded greatly. These developments enabled game designers to deliver state-of-the art graphics over the web. In 1997 the first of the massively multiplayer online role-playing (MMORP) games made its debut. *Ultima Online* enabled players to enter a fantasy world known as Britannia, where a civil war rages. In an MMORP game, players can make use of the Internet's social networking powers to interact with other players. Within three months, more than 50,000 players were paying subscription fees to play *Ultima Online*.

The Social Element of MMORP Games

The success of *Ultima Online* proved the enormous potential of MMORP games. Soon other MMORP games would make their debuts online, taking advantage of the improved graphics, more powerful microprocessor abilities, and faster connection speeds, giving players truly intense online experiences. Since 2002 the manufacturers of the Xbox, Wii, and PlayStation have introduced Internet-compatible versions of their consoles, enabling players to use those devices to participate in MMORP games. In 2009 the British-based media research firm Screen Digest estimated that online gamers in North America and Europe spend some $1.4 billion a year on subscription fees to play MMORP games such as *World of Warcraft*, *EverQuest*, and *Aion*. MMORP enthusiasts say they are drawn to the games because online gaming features a component that players do not find in the games they might play alone at home on their PlayStation, Xbox, or Wii consoles. When playing online, there is a social element—people can meet other players and develop online friendships.

> "[In *World of Warcraft*] you control a character who moves and reacts to commands in a stunningly realistic way. You move through an electronic fantasy world populated by other players, genuine people." [11]
>
> —*World of Warcraft* player Marty Toohey.

In MMORP games, players enter a world of fantasy or science fiction, assuming identities in which their avatars—virtual reality versions of themselves—interact with other players and match wits with adversaries. In *World of Warcraft*, players enter a mystical world known as Azeroth, where they encounter trolls, dragons, and other mythological creatures. Says *World of Warcraft* player Marty Toohey:

> For many people, it rivals their day-to-day . . . reality. You control a character who moves and reacts to commands in a stunningly realistic way. You move through an electronic fantasy world populated by other players, genuine people. Instead of dealing with plodding computer programs, you could be running alongside someone in Beijing. It's like a surrogate social life; an acquaintance of mine attended a wedding at which his friends (the bride and groom) had only seen his pixelated alter ego.[11]

The Birth of MP3

In the late 1970s, as game developers were taking their first tentative steps toward establishing an online gaming experience, a much different type of technology was under development at the University of Erlangen-Nuremberg in Germany. Engineers who specialized in audio technology were just beginning the long process of converting music into digital files. That technology, which would eventually become known as MP3, would dramatically change the music industry.

The audio engineers at Erlangen-Nuremberg worked under the leadership of Karlheinz Brandenburg, who started the project as part of his work toward a doctoral degree. It would take more than a dozen years before their research culminated in the digitalization of music. Indeed, as late as 1988, as the team was nearing success, Brandenburg remained unconvinced that the technology would amount to anything that might have consumer interest. "Somebody asked me what will become of this," Brandenburg recalled, "and I said it could just end up in libraries like so many other PhD theses."[12]

In 1991 the Erlangen-Nuremberg research team achieved a breakthrough by digitizing a complete song. The name of the song, which would make music history, was "Tom's Diner." The song had been a modest hit recorded by folksinger Suzanne Vega. The song lacked instrumentation—it was performed a cappella by Vega.

By then Brandenburg and his team had realized the commercial potential of what they had achieved. Also, by then, the Erlangen-Nuremberg engineers had learned they had competition—engineers at many large companies had also been working on the process. Although the Erlangen-Nuremberg engineers would ultimately be given most of the credit for developing MP3 technology, in all there were 14 different efforts under way to digitize music and make it available over the Internet.

In 1991 all 14 of those projects were submitted to an organization known as the Moving Picture Experts Group, or MPEG, a Geneva, Switzerland–based organization that sets international standards for digital media formats. Approval by MPEG was necessary to guarantee that every song would be digitized in the same format, ensuring they could be downloaded by any computer with Internet access. MPEG assessed all 14 projects and merged four of them into one format, calling it the MPEG-1 Audio Layer 3—or MP3 for short.

> **"A whole part of our culture is gone. We don't go out to record stores anymore on the weekends, and go through records and discover music that way. It's all online. . . . The whole process of being a music connoisseur is lost, which is sad."** [13]
>
> —Ian Drew, senior music editor for the magazine *Us Weekly*.

10 Billion Downloads

Since those early days of music digitization, MP3 technology has all but taken over the recording industry. Several companies sell songs as well as albums in MP3 formats; the largest provider of online songs is iTunes, which was launched by computer maker Apple in 2001. By 2009 Apple disclosed that some 75 million people had iTunes accounts. Moreover, account holders had their choice of more than 10 million songs from which to choose.

(Opposite) Apple's iPod (pictured) and its iTunes website and online store have transformed the music industry. Rather than buying CDs, millions of people around the world now download individual songs to their MP3 players.

While such statistics show MP3 technology has taken over the recording industry, some people are not sure the music business has changed for the better in the Internet age. Ian Drew, senior music editor for the magazine *Us Weekly*, says he grows nostalgic for the days when people spent hours in record stores, looking through the stacks of vinyl albums or even, in later years, CDs. He says:

> A whole part of our culture is gone. We don't go out to record stores anymore on the weekends, and go through records and discover music that way. It's all online. I mean, you YouTube something to find out if you want to hear it or not, real quick, you hear it and you download it instantly, and so people have it. The whole process of being a music connoisseur is lost, which is sad, but on the other hand, this is much easier than ever before.[13]

Nevertheless, critics like Drew know that MP3 is now the standard in the music industry, just as vinyl albums were the standard 50 years ago. The music industry has come a long way since the Erlangen-Nuremberg engineers began their research in the 1970s. So have the gaming and video industries, dramatically changing how people spend their leisure hours online.

Chapter Two

Does Online Gaming Isolate Players?

Paul Turner and Vicky Teather met online, which is not unusual because each day many people encounter one another on social networking sites or through online dating services or in Internet chat rooms. In their case, though, Turner and Teather, who live in Great Britain, met each other in the guise of mythological characters as they played the MMORP game *Final Fantasy*.

Turner had assumed the role of Andrus, a warrior clad in armor, while Teather's online character was Branwen, an elf with pointy ears and green hair. "One day, when as Andrus he endangered his own character in the game to save me, I felt an incredible bond between us," says Teather. "It might sound strange to people who have never played an online game, but the fact he was a traditional man with values to match and was protecting me was what first drew me to him."[14]

As with most adventures in *Final Fantasy* and similar MMORP games, the encounter between Andrus and Branwen had a storybook ending. Turner and Teather arranged to meet offline, and in 2010 they married.

While it is rare for MMORP players to develop relationships outside of their fantasy realms, the case of Turner and Teather illustrates that the online gaming world is opening new avenues for Internet users to interact socially. Says New York–based market research consultant Arnold Brown, "Clearly, the Internet has radically reshaped our social lives over the span of just a couple of decades, luring us into a virtual metaworld where traditional interactions—living, loving, belonging and separating . . . require new protocols."[15]

Over the past few years, plenty of people have been lured into the virtual worlds of *Final Fantasy, World of Warcraft,* and other MMORP games. According to comScore, a Reston, Virginia, market research firm, nearly 86 million Americans played online games in 2008—a 27 percent hike over the number of Americans who played games the year before. Worldwide, comScore reported that 217 million people spend time online playing games. Says a statement by the company: "With one in four Internet users visiting a gaming site, playing games online is extremely popular. The fact that these websites are pulling in over a quarter of the total worldwide Internet population shows what a global phenomenon gaming has become."[16]

The Dark Side of Gaming

But there is also a dark side of Internet gaming. Some gamers find themselves so immersed in their online fantasy worlds that they lose touch with the real world. They stop working, drop out of school, stop seeing

Multiplayer online gaming has opened new avenues for Internet users to interact socially, but some gamers become so immersed in their online fantasy worlds that they lose touch with daily life. Final Fantasy, *shown here at a screening, is one of the online multiplayer games that has a large and loyal following.*

friends, and even neglect eating and personal hygiene. Allen, a *World of Warcraft* player from Canada, is a typical case. His wife, Kristan, told *Maclean's* magazine that her husband's devotion to *World of Warcraft* has caused him to neglect the couple's three young children. She says: "They ask him to go to the park. He'll say, 'If I get off [the computer] I'll die.' They'll build Lego castles to impress him—they're lucky to get a nod. If it were up to him, he'd take a family photo with the damn game by his side."[17]

The state-of-the-art graphics, complicated scenarios, and emotional attachments players develop for their avatars all serve to make online gaming into an intensely engrossing experience. It is not unusual for players to spend several hours a day playing *Second Life*, *EverQuest*, *World of Warcraft*, and other MMORP games. And because of the high level of concentration required to play the games, players may often find themselves ignoring all that is happening in the real world away from their screens.

> "It might sound strange to people who have never played an online game, but the fact he was a traditional man with values to match and was protecting me was what first drew me to him."[14]
>
> —Vicky Teather, who met her future husband during online game playing.

Indeed, there is more to the online gaming experience than simply playing the game. For many of the popular MMORP games, devoted players often create their own "fansites," providing news and gossip related to the game and its designers. Fansites may also provide hints and strategies for play, assistance in designing avatars, and access to software patches, which can be downloaded to alter or enhance the gaming environment. Some fansites provide blogs, giving players opportunities to exchange ideas and find guidance from more experienced players who take on the roles of mentors. Some MMORP fansites even charge subscription fees.

Therefore, truly devoted online gamers do not only spend time online playing their games, they also make frequent visits to their favorite fansites to pick up tips on play and to keep abreast of the latest developments in the game. Wrote *Hardware* magazine, a digital media journal: "The success of MMORP games today depends a lot on the dedication of the players who patronize the service. Fansites, mentors, integration of the game with other web services and team building are some of the characteristics of a good MMORP experience for any player."[18]

Devotion to the Game

Dedicated MMORP players must not only learn the rules of the game but the game's nuances as well. Matt Barton points out that the designers of the MMORP game *Legend of Faerghail* have instilled female characters with greater powers of wisdom while male characters are endowed with greater physical strength. Players who do not catch on to these nuances may find themselves struggling to compete on a high level.

In addition, the designers of *Legend of Faerghail* have also invented no fewer than eight languages—players need to learn these languages if they expect to interact and compete with other players. Even after learning the rules of *Legend of Faerghail*, nuances of the game, and languages of the characters, the competitor must then figure out how to win. "The goal of the game is to learn why the normally peaceful elves have suddenly turned violent," explains Barton. "Naturally, this simple quest soon spirals into a much thicker plot."[19]

Of course, learning all one needs to know about playing *Legend of Faerghail* and similar games takes a lot of devotion, study, and time—all of which have to be squeezed into a normal life. Allen, the Canadian father of three, arrives home from work at 6:00 p.m. each night, then, after a quick dinner, sits down in front of his computer screen, where he will play *World of Warcraft* until midnight. On weekends, it is not unusual for Allen to play from 9:00 a.m. to 2:00 a.m. Is it any wonder, then, that players like Allen are accused of neglecting their families? "Am I thinking about divorce?" asks Allen's wife, Kristan. "Hell, yeah."[20]

"The success of MMORP games today depends a lot on the dedication of the players who patronize the service. Fansites, mentors, integration of the game with other web services and team building are some of the characteristics of a good MMORP experience for any player."[18]

—*Hardware* magazine, a digital media journal.

The Importance of MMORP Rankings

Back in the 1970s, at the dawn of the video game age, virtually the only places where games could be played were bars, bowling alleys, and pinball arcades. In the era before the Internet as well as home consoles and computers, players had no choice other than to pour quarters into the machines in order to play the games.

One of the great motivations for this style of play, however, was the ability to record one's initials on the screen after registering a high score. Typically, it took a top-10 score to be given the honor of dialing in one's initials on the game's hall of fame screen.

Today's online games feature a similar attraction: Players are ranked, and those rankings are made available on the Internet, often recorded on fansites. Some players acknowledge that achieving fame by scoring a high ranking is a major lure of the game and the reason they spend hours at play. Says Sameer Salji, a student at Ryerson University in Toronto, Canada, "If I didn't play so much I'd lose my rank, and you don't want that because you work so hard." Salji admits to playing MMORP games as long as 12 hours a day, mostly to maintain his high ranking.

Quoted in Cynthia Reynolds, "Videogame Widows," *Maclean's*, January 16, 2006, p. 42.

More at Ease in a Virtual World

Allen was not always so devoted to *World of Warcraft*. According to his wife, before he discovered the game, he was an avid soccer player and bicycle rider. In other words, he was in all other respects a normal young adult who enjoyed engaging in social activities with friends. Many MMORP players turn to the games, though, specifically because they do not enjoy social interactions with others: People annoy them, and therefore they would rather interact with avatars in a virtual world.

Zach Elliott serves as an example of somebody who finds himself more at home in a virtual world than in a world where he has to interact with others. A husband and father from Wisconsin, Elliott says he has no qualms about spending three hours or more a day in his basement playing the MMORP game *Final Fantasy*. He enjoys life in a virtual world, he says, because he does not have to put up with characters he finds annoying. The game features a "blacklist" command that enables him to block out other players who get on his nerves. "It's something I wish I had in real life," he says. "There are people in this game who irritate me unbelievably."[21]

Mental health experts wonder whether eschewing relationships with others in favor of online game playing is healthy. They point out that in the real world, there is no blacklist command, meaning that people have to learn to interact with others even though they may find them annoying. To escape that type of responsibility, mental health professionals suggest that some people will find reasons to spend more time in their virtual worlds and less time interacting with real people. "We are seeing more and more adults and adolescents struggling with real world relationships because of virtual world relationships they have created,"[22] says Eric Zehr, president of behavioral services at the Illinois Institute for Addiction Recovery in Peoria, Illinois.

> "We are seeing more and more adults and adolescents struggling with real world relationships because of virtual world relationships they have created."[22]
>
> —Eric Zehr, president of behavioral services at the Illinois Institute for Addiction Recovery.

A counselor at the institute, Libby Smith, recalls the case of one client, a man in his mid-twenties who dropped out of college so he could spend more time playing *World of Warcraft*. His devotion to the game cost him his girlfriend, Smith says, and yet the client insists that there is nothing wrong with living in a virtual world. "He maintains he has no problem,"[23] Smith says. The man agreed to seek counseling at the institute only after family members intervened.

High Rates of Depression

People who glue themselves to their computer screens, avoiding contact with real people in favor of characters in a virtual world, may be afflicted with depression, which is a mental illness. Depressed people are frequently sad; other symptoms include chronic fatigue, insomnia, changes in appetite, agitation, pessimism, and thoughts of suicide.

Online gamers fill an Internet café in China. In addition to playing their favorite games, serious gamers often devote additional hours to searching the Web for tips and tricks that will help them defeat their opponents.

Scientific studies are starting to show that online game players suffer higher rates of depression than people who do not play MMORP games. A 2009 study by Northwestern University in Illinois found that in a survey of 7,000 online *EverQuest* players, the depression rate was 30 percent among those who played several hours day. Among those who do not play MMORP games, the depression rate is 21 percent. Researchers are not sure why online game players suffer from depression more than others. They speculate that online players may find themselves emotionally drawn into their experiences, and when they are unable to resolve conflicts they encounter online, they know few people to whom they can turn for support. As a result, they keep their frustrations bottled up inside and grow depressed.

One former *World of Warcraft* player, Northwestern University student Kevin Ryan, says he can appreciate how MMORP players may grow so emotionally attached to their avatars that they could slip into frustration and despondence if things do not go their way online. Playing an MMORP game is a much different experience, he says, than playing a video game on a home console—in which players do not generally develop emotional attachments to the game characters. He says:

> You usually play a game, sit down and beat it, but with *World of Warcraft* you're immersed entirely in a dynamic world. The fact that you're able to develop a character of something that slices dragons is kind of intense. You kind of get addicted . . . because you start to identify with the character you create. You take it through the long grueling process of [playing the game] instead of just shooting things in the head for a half hour on an Xbox.[24]

Self-Destructive Behavior

The Northwestern University researchers also speculated that more MMORP players exhibit higher rates of depression because depressed people may be more likely than others to be drawn to the online gaming experience: Unable to find happiness in real-life emotional relationships, they seek it in make-believe characters.

Although Turner and Teather—the British *Final Fantasy* players who arranged to meet offline and then married—found happiness in real life, there have also been other, darker stories reported about MMORP gamers in recent years. Indeed, depressed people are more likely than others to engage in self-destructive behavior—including suicide. In 2002, 21-year-old *EverQuest* player Shawn Woolley committed suicide, evidently out of frustration over an experience while playing the game. "He couldn't stay off it," says his mother, Elizabeth Woolley. "That's how strong that game is. You can't just get up and walk away. . . . He was so upset. And then I

Do Women Play Online Games?

The stereotypical image many people have of the online game player is that of a teenage boy or young adult male. Demographic studies of Internet game players prove those images to be false. According to a study by comScore, a Reston, Virginia–based market research firm, nearly half of all US online game players are female.

The company's report shows that in 2008, 85 million Americans played online games, including 42 million women between the ages of 12 and 64. The fastest growing segment of female game players are members of the 12–17 age group. The number of female players in that age group rose 55 percent between August 2007 and August 2008.

A typical player is Chandra Smith, a 24-year-old mother from Kirby, Texas, who says she started playing online games as a way of bonding with her husband. Says Smith, "There have been times that I'll sign on to it and I'll play for what I think is an hour and I'll look up and it's been four or five hours."

Quoted in Kalyn Belsha, "Video Games Not Just for Dudes, Dude," *Beaumont (TX) Enterprise*, August 22, 2010.

was trying to talk to him about it, and I said, 'Well, Shawn, you know, those aren't people—they're not real people.' He was so upset. I mean, he wasn't angry, he was hurt."[25]

Meanwhile, in Beijing, China, the parents of 13-year-old Zhang Xiaoyi attribute their son's 2004 suicide to his belief that he had actually entered the world of *Warcraft: Orcs and Humans* (a variation of *World of Warcraft*)—believing he could fly. Zhang took his own life by jumping from the roof of the 24-story apartment building where he lived.

He left behind a note that said he wanted "to join the heroes of the game he worshipped."[26] The boy's family retained a Beijing attorney to pursue a legal case against the Chinese company that administers *Warcraft: Orcs and Humans*. Said the lawyer, Zhang Chunliang, "Just as power plants must take responsibility for discharging pollutants, game companies should take responsibility for the consequences of spiritual pollution caused by their products."[27]

In Defense of Gaming

Despite the evidence produced by the Northwestern University study as well as the real-life tragedies in the cases of Woolley and Zhang, many experts disagree with the notion that online game playing makes people depressed or otherwise ruins their relationships with friends and family members. Henry Jenkins, a professor of comparative studies at the Massachusetts Institute of Technology, argues that rather than isolating people, online game playing can bring people together. He says people who may otherwise be lonely or socially awkward can find an online community of others who share the common interest of playing games.

Moreover, Jenkins says, game playing helps participants learn how to follow rules as well as the consequences of breaking the rules. Says Jenkins: "In this way there are really two games taking place simultaneously: one, the explicit conflict and combat on the screen; the other, the implicit cooperation and comradeship between the players. Two players may be fighting to death on screen and growing closer as friends off screen."[28]

Another proponent of online gaming is James Bower, a neuroscientist at the University of Texas. Bower points out that unlike the so-called first-person shooter games played on home video game consoles, online games engage participants and hold their attentions for longer spans of time. It is a much more productive use of brain power, he says, than simply participating in a virtual gun battle every few seconds on a home console. Bower adds:

> One of the things you're seeing, I think, is that smart games—games that involve your actually being able to learn something that gives you an advantage in the social structure—are becoming more interesting and powerful games. The point is, when games are built assuming that humans have a two-minute attention span, players stay there for about two minutes. The games that drive longer involvement . . . involve your actually having to be intelligent and learn something to play them.[29]

Expressing Individuality

Online game playing is also defended by University of North Carolina computer scientist Tiffany Barnes, who says MMORP games provide players with opportunities to express their individuality—another factor that is largely missing from video games played on home consoles. In addition, she says, games played on home consoles usually have a set goal that all players have to meet—in most cases defeating an adversary. In contrast, MMORP games enable players to participate at their own skill levels and achieve outcomes that may differ from player to player. "You can set your own goals with games now, so they're just a whole different kind of medium," she says. "So someone who says you're going to lose your individuality with games is just not playing games."[30]

> "He couldn't stay off it. That's how strong that game is. You can't just get up and walk away."[25]
>
> —Elizabeth Woolley, whose son Shawn committed suicide after playing *EverQuest*.

Another defender of online gaming is the author of the Northwestern University study, behavioral sciences professor Noshir Contractor. Even though the study indicated a hike in the rates of depression among online game players, Contractor believes there may also be therapeutic value in the games, providing people with an outlet for their aggressions. It is the role-playing component, he says, that may provide the most therapeutic value.

In a virtual universe, Contractor says, players may permit themselves to display aggressive tendencies or other emotions that they would never permit themselves to assume in the real world. "When they start playing the game, they take on the role of someone in the 12th century and talk like them and behave like them, and everything they say and do is not who they are, but within the character," Contractor says. "Based on . . . interviews [MMORP games] seem like a therapeutic approach."[31]

Gamer Widows

Whether the games cause depression or provide a measure of therapeutic value to the players, there is no question that a lot of family members find themselves isolated from husbands, wives, fathers, and mothers who spend hours a day playing games online. Sherry Myrow, a resident of Toronto, Canada, found herself isolated from her game-playing husband who, soon after their wedding, discovered *World of Warcraft*. "I only saw happiness in his eyes if he was playing the game or talking about the game,"[32] she says.

Myrow wondered whether other spouses were also being neglected by husbands and wives, so she started a support group, GamerWidow.com, to reach out to others who have found themselves in similar situations. Soon after establishing the website in 2005, membership grew to more than 4,000 neglected spouses.

Members who have been drawn to the site share experiences and help each other cope with spouses who devote many of their waking hours to *World of Warcraft*, *Second Life*, *EverQuest*, and similar games. Some of the comments posted on Myrow's website include:

> He discovered *Second Life* earlier this year. I don't know this person. . . .

> We have been together more than 10 years. . . .We hardly ever argued, agreed on everything . . . life was great. Now . . . there is no life.

> In the beginning, he played around the clock, took time off work, stopped eating and drinking and caring about anything. I truly believe he lost touch with reality.[33]

As those comments would seem to indicate, there are many people who feel neglected because their loved ones spend excessive amounts of time glued to their computer screens, immersed deep inside the fantasy worlds of MMORP games. Clearly, those players have isolated themselves from friends, family members, classmates, and coworkers. As the

> "You can set your own goals with games now, so they're just a whole different kind of medium. So someone who says you're going to lose your individuality with games is just not playing games."[30]
>
> —University of North Carolina computer scientist Tiffany Barnes.

Northwestern University study indicates, evidence has surfaced suggesting that such devotion to online gaming could lead to mental illness. Gaming does have its defenders, though, who insist that the online experience does have some positive impacts—providing people with outlets for their aggressions or letting them explore personality traits they would not ordinarily expose in the real world.

Regardless of how much time individual gamers spend at their computer screens, the statistics indicate that gaming is a growing presence on the Internet. More people than ever are now playing online games—a fact that their friends and family members may simply have to get used to.

Chapter Three

Can Online Entertainment Be Addictive?

Most poker players are well aware of the term *tilt*. Players who find themselves in the throes of a tilt have had runs of particularly bad luck. After losing hand after hand, they make bizarre bets on what they would otherwise recognize as bad cards. But they are so far behind that they are willing to make chancy wagers in an effort to recoup their losses. Players on tilts rarely get even. Mostly, they just lose more money.

Greg Hogan Jr. was in the throes of the worst tilt of his life. The student at Lehigh University in Bethlehem, Pennsylvania, spent hours each night in his dorm room, playing poker online. Mostly, he had been losing and found himself running up a credit card debt of $7,500. "The side of me that said, 'Just one more hand,' was the side that always won," he says. "I couldn't get away from it, not until all my money was gone."[34]

Hogan was addicted to online gambling. It had consumed his life, affected his studies, and forced him into debt. And yet, he returned night after night to his computer screen, wagering sums he knew he could not afford playing poker on the Internet.

On December 9, 2005, Hogan and two friends went to the movies. On their way to the theater, Hogan asked to stop at a bank so he could cash a check. As his two friends waited in the car, Hogan entered the bank and passed a note to the teller advising the woman that he was armed (which he was not) and demanding money. The stunned teller handed over nearly $3,000. Hogan quietly returned to the car, and the three friends continued their trip to the movies.

After returning to campus, Hogan used some of the money to help pay off his gambling debts—he had borrowed hundreds of dollars from his fraternity buddies. But it did not take long for police to track him down—a witness had jotted down the license plate number of the car in which Hogan was riding. Hours after robbing the bank, police caught up with him. After his arrest he quickly confessed and was sentenced to 22 months in prison.

100 Hands per Hour

Hogan had turned into a degenerate gambler thanks mostly to the Internet. Too young to gain admission to casinos, Hogan had no trouble creating accounts with online gambling sites. He is not alone: An estimated 1.6 million college students gamble online, according to the Philadelphia-based Annenberg Public Policy Center, and many of them suffer gambling addictions. Says Neda Faregh, a professor of health psychology

Unlike a casual poker night with friends—which might include friendly bluffing, food and drink, and low stakes—online poker can be serious business. Players can quickly accumulate thousands of dollars in debts.

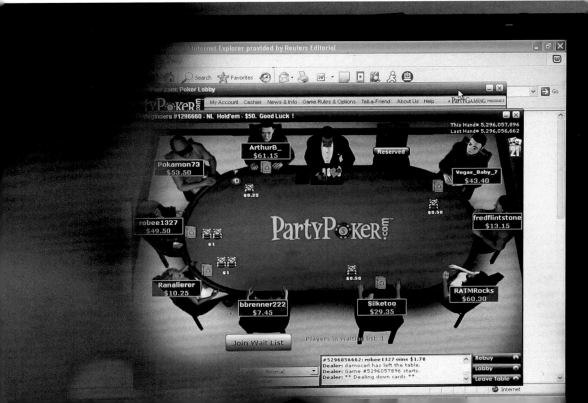

at McGill University in Canada: "For adolescent gamblers in particular, the risk of developing pathological gambling is almost twice [that of] the adult population. They're more vulnerable to the negative consequences of gambling."[35] Adds McGill researcher Jeffrey Derevensky, "The kids really think they can log on and become the next world champion."[36]

The poker games played online are a lot different than the games a group of friends might play around the kitchen table. Most casual poker players enjoy the camaraderie of being with friends—the exchange of jokes and gossip, the friendly bluffing, the sandwiches or snacks. Poker night in a friend's kitchen may last a couple of hours. Meanwhile, the stakes are often modest. Perhaps a dozen or more hands might be dealt during the course of the evening, and few players go home with much more money—or less money—than they brought to the game.

In online poker, though, there are no friends to bluff and no gossip or jokes to exchange. There is not even a break while the dealer shuffles the cards. The virtual cards are dealt rapid-fire. In Hogan's case it was not unusual for him to play as many as 100 hands an hour. "Internet poker induces a trancelike state," says Derevensky. "The player loses all track of time, where they are, what they're doing."[37]

Hogan's losses were significant, but Derevensky says other young people have lost much more. Derevensky says he once helped break the gambling addiction of a 17-year-old boy who had lost $30,000 wagering on an online poker site. One young gambler, who was interviewed by the *New York Times*, claimed to have lost $250,000 playing poker online. "It fried my brain," the young gambler told the newspaper. "I would roll out of bed, go to my computer and stay there for 20 hours. One night after I went to sleep, my dad called. I woke up instantly, picked up the phone and said, 'I raise.'"[38]

Craps, Roulette, Slots, and Sports Betting

Online gambling is not limited to poker. Players who do not know the rules of poker or simply just doubt their skills at the game can find other forms of gambling available online. Online casinos offer wagering on craps and roulette, which are largely games of chance that require few skills. Requiring no skill to play whatsoever are online slot machines.

Surfing the Web at Work

Addiction to Internet entertainment can affect a worker's productivity. According to a 2008 report issued by Livigent, a Romanian-based web security firm, as much as 40 percent of Internet use on an office computer is not work related. "[An] interesting statistic is that the younger the employee is, the more time he or she is wasting," said the Livigent report. "Apparently, those who are 56 years or older spend as much as 30 minutes per day on personal [Internet] activities, while those 25 and younger waste about 2 hours daily."

Some experts believe that giving employees breaks during the day to surf the web actually enhances productivity. They liken Internet breaks to coffee breaks—brief periods in the morning and afternoon in which workers are given time away from their jobs. A 2011 University of Copenhagen study found that workers who were given time off from their jobs to view humorous online videos were sharper and made fewer mistakes than other workers.

Livigent, "The Modern Approach to Employees' Internet Usage," 2008. www.livigent.com.

While these games may be easy to play, the odds are stacked in favor of the house because the payoffs are, on average, less than the fees charged to play.

Certainly, a lucky player can walk away from an online casino with a profit after an evening of playing virtual roulette, but in the long run the casino will be the winner because most players will bet more than they win. Still, even though the odds are stacked in the website casino's favor, players still find the games enticing, and many play. According to an estimate by the accounting firm PriceWaterhouseCoopers, online gamblers worldwide wagered $144 billion in 2011.

In addition to poker, roulette, craps, and similar games, a very popular form of online gambling is making bets on sporting events—particularly professional and college football games. One study cited by ABC News found that $7 billion is wagered online each year on a single game—the Super Bowl. And when football is out of season, on-line gamblers can find action on many other types of sporting events, particularly horse racing and college basketball.

As with most types of online gambling, sports betting on the Internet can be highly addictive. One gambler who found himself swallowed up by the addiction was Mark Erickson, an accountant from Phoenix, Arizona. "I've heard other people compare it to a cocaine addiction, the high you get from that, and that's the euphoria I felt," he says. "It becomes an all-consuming activity: The lining up the money, the handicapping of the game, the betting of the game, the watching of the game. Win or lose, it didn't matter to me, it just set me up to bet again."[39]

It did not take long for Erickson to place bets he could not afford to cover. In a very short time, he ran up gambling debts of some $400,000. To pay off the online bookies, Erickson was forced to steal from his clients. When his clients discovered the thefts, Erickson fled—running away from his debts as well as his family members. While in hiding, Erickson considered taking his own life.

Instead of committing suicide, Erickson returned home and admitted to the thefts. He served a prison term and hopes his experience will provide a warning to others who make sports bets over the Internet. Experts hope others do pay heed to Erickson's story, but they also acknowledge that it is very likely many other gamblers will make the same mistakes as Erickson. Says Ed Looney, executive director of the New Jersey Council on Compulsive Gambling: "[Sports betting] is American, like apple pie. That will always be there. People love to bet on [sports]. People love to bet on their football games."[40]

> **"The side of me that said, 'Just one more hand,' was the side that always won. I couldn't get away from it, not until all my money was gone."[34]**
>
> —Greg Hogan Jr., whose addiction to Internet gambling prompted him to rob a bank.

Different Rewards for Gamers

Online gambling may be addictive, but other forms of entertainment found on the Internet can also be addictive. Indeed, the reason that MMORP games sometimes lead to social isolation is because they are highly addictive. Even as players fail their classes, drop out of school, quit their jobs, lose friends, and otherwise isolate themselves, they cannot seem to pull themselves away from their screens.

For online game players, the rewards are not the same as those chased by online gamblers. Instead of pursuing wealth, addicted online gamers merely seek the satisfaction of beating their virtual opponents or scoring points.

For addicted gamers, that is more than enough enticement: Some have refused to leave their screens for days at a time. In Sweden, for example, a 15-year-old boy suffered an epileptic seizure after spending 24 hours straight playing *World of Warcraft* with his friends. "They played all day and all night," his father told the British newspaper the *Telegraph*. "Maybe they got a few hours sleep. They ate a little food and breakfast at their computers."[41]

Horses fly around the track at the Kentucky Derby at Churchill Downs in Louisville. Online gambling—which entails betting on sporting events such as football, basketball, and horse racing—can be addictive.

Even casual gamers admit that MMORP games can have addictive qualities. In Ohio, Kent State University student Connor Shivers says he may play for as long as four hours a day. "It's very hard to let go because you are chasing the next reward,"[42] he says.

Withdrawal Symptoms

Mental health professionals believe that people who are addicted to on-line gaming or gambling are not that much different from people who suffer addictions to cigarettes, drugs, and other vices. And just like nicotine addicts or heroin addicts, online addicts who give up their addictions may find themselves suffering withdrawal symptoms. They may become physically ill or emotionally despondent: They become so depressed they cannot rise from their beds in the morning.

Craig Smallwood, a 51-year-old Hawaiian man, found himself addicted to the MMORP game *Lineage II*. Smallwood believes he spent more than 10 hours a day playing the game over the course of five years.

"Internet poker induces a trancelike state. The player loses all track of time, where they are, what they're doing."[37]

—McGill University addictions researcher Jeffrey Derevensky.

After several occasions in which he broke the rules, NCsoft Corporation, the South Korean company that administers the game, barred him from playing. Cut off cold turkey from *Lineage II*, Smallwood fell into a deep depression. He suffered severe paranoia, meaning he manifested delusional beliefs, and also started hallucinating. Finally, Smallwood had to be hospitalized for three weeks.

In 2010 Smallwood sued NCsoft Corporation, alleging that *Lineage II* should be packaged with a warning label explaining the addictive powers of the game—just as cigarette packs carry labels warning of the addictive nature of tobacco. Smallwood's case is not likely to be resolved for several years.

Internet Addiction Disorder

Smallwood's assertion that he was addicted to Internet gaming did not surprise mental health experts. During the 1990s, an era when faster

Internet speeds and more powerful computers became available to consumers, mental health experts started noticing how the online world was
affecting dedicated web surfers. In 2008 the *American Journal of Psychiatry* recognized Internet addiction disorder (IAD) as a mental illness. Says
Ronald Pies, a professor of psychiatry at the State University of New
York in Syracuse, "From what we know, many so-called 'Internet addicts'
are folks who have severe depression, anxiety disorders, or social phobic
symptoms that make it hard for them to live a full, balanced life and deal
face-to-face with other people."[43]

According to Kimberly Young, director of the Center for Internet Addiction Recovery in Bradford, Pennsylvania, symptoms of IAD include:

- Failed attempts to control behavior
- Heightened sense of euphoria while involved in computer and In-
  ternet activities
- Neglecting friends and family
- Neglecting sleep to stay online
- Being dishonest with others
- Feeling guilty, ashamed, anxious, or depressed as a result of online
  behavior
- Physical changes such as weight gain or loss, backaches, headaches
  and carpal tunnel syndrome, a chronic soreness in the wrists
- Withdrawing from other pleasurable activities

Young says an addiction to the Internet manifests itself in traits that
are similar to those found in addictions to drugs, alcohol, tobacco, and
other substances. She says,

> If you're more interested in spending time with the thing you're
> addicted to than you are with your family and friends, then that's
> a symptom. If you're preoccupied with the thing you're addicted
> to, then that's a symptom. Those things are the same for any ad-
> diction. Internet addiction can lead to more serious symptoms,
> including health problems from a lack of sun or exercise, increased
> senses of loneliness and depression and the loss of social skills. If
> left untreated, Internet addictions can increase the likelihood that
> the individual will get divorced or fired, or have financial [and]
> academic . . . problems. Internet addictions can be very serious.[44]

Internet Addiction in South Korea

South Korea has the fastest broadband in the world, meaning that computers in South Korea can process more information in faster times than in any other country on earth. In addition, South Koreans pay some of the lowest rates in the world for Internet access. In South Korea the average monthly bill to connect to the Internet is $28.50. In the United States the average monthly fee is $45.50.

But the South Koreans have paid a price for cheaper and faster Internet service. The average South Korean teenager spends 23 hours a week playing online games. Meanwhile, the government has estimated that more than 200,000 South Korean young people suffer from Internet addiction disorder.

In 2010 the press in South Korea reported the tragic story of an infant girl who starved to death because both of her parents were Internet addicts. The parents spent most of their free time playing an MMORP game and often forgot to feed their daughter.

In response to the growing Internet addiction problem in South Korea, the government has directed online gaming sites to shut off access to young people between the hours of midnight and 8:00 a.m. Meanwhile, more than 100 clinics that specialize in treating Internet addiction have opened in the country.

Pornography on the Internet

Internet addiction is not limited to playing MMORP games and gambling. Young says many people are addicted to spending time on social networking sites like Facebook or shopping on online auction sites like eBay. Others are simply what she calls compulsive surfers.

And, certainly, there are many people who are addicted to Internet pornography. According to the advocacy group SafeFamiles.org, as many as 10 percent of adult Internet users may be addicted to cyberporn—and not all of them are men. The organization reports that 28 percent of Internet pornography addicts are women.

A 43-year-old Internet pornography addict named Brad told *Ladies' Home Journal* that he spent many hours each day glued in front of a computer in his basement, trawling through pornographic websites. Said Brad, "Cybersex became the most important thing in my life."[45]

One day, Brad's wife discovered his Internet addiction—he had inadvertently left the computer on, displaying a pornographic image on the screen. The couple's marriage nearly ended that day, but Brad agreed to seek psychotherapy and now believes he has kicked his Internet pornography habit.

Mental health experts suggest that addiction to Internet pornography can have many wide-ranging effects on people's lives. In addition to effects associated with other forms of Internet addiction—such as isolating people from their professional or academic responsibilities as well as from friends and family members—an addiction to Internet pornography can promote twisted notions of how to maintain romantic relationships. Indeed, constant exposure to Internet pornography can lead to aggressive and belligerent behavior. Write psychologists Hal Arkowitz and Scott O. Lilienfeld:

> "From what we know, many so-called 'Internet addicts' are folks who have severe depression, anxiety disorders, or social phobic symptoms that make it hard for them to live a full, balanced life and deal face-to-face with other people."[43]
>
> —Ronald Pies, professor of psychiatry at the State University of New York in Syracuse.

Numerous studies have found associations between the amount of exposure to pornography and sexually belligerent attitudes such as endorsing coercive sex and sexually aggressive behaviors—say, forcibly holding a woman down. These associations are strongest for men who watch violent pornography and for those who already tend to be sexually aggressive.

Other findings have tied frequent porn use to attitudes such as assigning blame to victims of sexual assault, justifying the actions of sexual predators, and discounting the violence of rape. Enthusiasm for porn often accompanies callousness toward women, dissatisfaction with a partner's sexual performance and appearance, and doubts about the value of marriage. Such attitudes are clearly detrimental to relationships with women and could conceivably be linked to crimes against them.[46]

Among those who have admitted to a dedication to online pornography is singer John Mayer. In an interview, Mayer said: "You wake up in the morning, open a thumbnail page, and it leads to a Pandora's box of visuals. . . . Twenty seconds ago you thought that photo was the hottest thing you ever saw, but you throw it back and continue your . . . hunt and continue to make yourself late for work. How does that not affect the psychology of having a relationship with somebody? It's got to."[47]

Finding Help for Internet Addictions

People who suffer addictions to Internet pornography as well as Internet gaming and gambling do have places to turn for aid. Mental health professionals have crafted treatments for IAD. The first clinic established specifically to treat IAD is known as reSTART, located in Fall City, Washington.

> "Twenty seconds ago you thought that photo was the hottest thing you ever saw, but you throw it back and continue your . . . hunt and continue to make yourself late for work. How does that not affect the psychology of having a relationship with somebody? It's got to."[47]
>
> —Singer John Mayer, discussing his devotion to Internet pornography.

The clinic's first patient was Ben Alexander, a college student who was forced to leave the University of Iowa after just one semester due to poor grades.

The reason Alexander failed all his courses was simple: He never went to class, preferring to spend all his time in his dorm room playing *World of Warcraft*. "At first, I played only a couple of hours a day," he says. "But in less than two months, I was playing 16 or 17 hours a day. I often fell asleep at my computer keyboard at night."[48]

To help their son kick his Internet habit, in 2009 Alexander's parents enrolled him in reSTART, which is run by psychotherapists

Musician John Mayer, performing here in 2011, has publicly admitted to having a devotion to online pornography. One organization estimates that 10 percent of adult Internet users are addicted to cyberporn.

Hilarie Cash and Cosette Dawna Rae. The 45-day program does not permit Internet addicts access to a computer. Rather, the patients must learn to restructure their lives away from the online world. Soon after arriving at the clinic, denied access to the Internet, Alexander started suffering withdrawal symptoms. "I was depressed, irritable, and very anxious,"[49] he says.

To wean their client off his Internet gaming addiction, Cash and Rae filled Alexander's days with activities to keep him busy. He was given carpentry projects to perform and also given responsibility for caring for some chickens and goats that are kept on the clinic's property. Physical fitness is also a priority at the clinic—Alexander became an avid runner during his 45 days of treatment. He also spent time in daily counseling sessions with the two psychotherapists, discussing his goals in life and how to achieve them.

> **"I was depressed, irritable, and very anxious."[49]**
>
> —College student Ben Alexander describing his Internet withdrawal symptoms.

Mostly, the two psychotherapists filled up Alexander's days with activities that kept him busy and prevented him from lapsing into periods of boredom—times when he would feel inclined to lose himself in the fantasy world of online gaming. By the end of the 45-day session, Alexander pronounced himself cured of Internet addiction. "I don't think I'll be going back to *World of Warcraft* anytime soon,"[50] he says.

Degrees of Addiction

Many people who suffer from Internet addictions harm themselves and others. Hogan and Erickson ended up in prison, while Smallwood had to be hospitalized. Alexander had to put his college career on hold while he kicked the Internet gaming habit with the help of professional psychotherapists.

All of these former Internet addicts have seen their lives improve after giving up online gambling and gaming. Sadly, others are making the same mistakes—spending all their time online, making wagers they cannot afford, neglecting their work or studies for the thrills of outscoring a rival in an MMORP game, or winning a hand in an online poker tournament. Whether those players suffer the same fates as Hogan, Erickson, Smallwood, and Alexander depends largely on the hold the Internet has over their lives.

Chapter Four

Can Online Entertainment Be Regulated?

Boston University student Joel Tenenbaum is a fan of Green Day and Aerosmith. To obtain music for those groups and others, Tenenbaum made use of software he obtained through the file-sharing website Kazaa. "He was a kid who did what kids do and loved technology and loved music,"[51] says Charles Nesson, Tenenbaum's lawyer.

File sharing, also known as peer-to-peer or P2P, has been a staple of the Internet since its earliest days. In simple terms P2P facilitates the ability of two users to share content. At first, computer engineers made use of P2P to exchange software, but soon consumers found resources through file sharing. Games, music and video all became available to Internet users who make use of P2P.

The main problem with P2P, though, is that it enables users to skirt copyright laws. Copyright is the legal protection provided to the producers of so-called intellectual content, enabling them to be guaranteed exclusive financial rewards for their efforts. Copyrights have helped protect authors and other producers of intellectual content since colonial times. In 1997 Congress extended copyright law specifically to the Internet when it adopted the No Electronic Theft Act, commonly known as the NET Act.

In addition to authors, others who benefit from copyright protection are publishers of books, producers of music and movies, and designers of video games. In other words, every time somebody buys a CD at a music store, a percentage of the sale is paid to the artist in the form of a royalty. However, every time a song is downloaded through a P2P connection, the user does not pay a fee, and therefore the artist does not receive a royalty payment. Says a statement by the RIAA: "Who pays when music is stolen? Singers, songwriters, musicians, album producers, audio engineers, sound technicians, recording studio managers, and many others that contribute to creating the music we love, and who depend on a healthy industry for their jobs and their families' income."[52]

Tenenbaum needed a lawyer because he is alleged to have downloaded songs with the help of P2P software he obtained through Kazaa and therefore did not pay royalties to the artists and producers. The RIAA elected to sue Tenenbaum, contending that he cheated several artists,

A shopper browses the CD shelves in a Los Angeles music store. When people buy CDs, a percentage of the sale goes to the musicians in the form of royalties. When songs are downloaded illegally through peer-to-peer file sharing, the musicians do not receive that compensation.

songwriters, music producers, and others out of royalties. In 2009 a jury agreed and ordered Tenenbaum to pay damages of $675,000 to the artists and producers of 30 songs he had downloaded from the Internet. Later, a judge reduced the damages to $67,500. Still, the damages may prove to be a tremendous burden on Tenenbaum. (By 2011 he was still appealing the fine.) "The music industry is acting like a digital police force,"[53] complained Nesson.

Like the Wild West

Tenenbaum's case illustrates that the Internet is, in many regards, a lot like the Wild West. It is essentially a lawless place where thievery is common.

> "Who pays when music is stolen? Singers, songwriters, musicians, album producers, audio engineers, sound technicians, recording studio managers, and many others that contribute to creating the music we love."[52]
>
> —Recording Industry Association of America.

Over the years efforts to regulate content on the Internet have largely failed. In 1996 Congress passed the Communications Decency Act. It was an attempt by the federal government to deny access by minors to pornographic websites. The courts soon threw out the law, finding that it was so broad that it could apply to virtually any form of expression and was therefore in violation of the First Amendment right of free speech. A later law, the Children's Internet Protection Act of 2001, does require schools and public libraries to place filters on computers to prevent children from accessing pornographic sites. Although there are state and federal measures that strictly enforce laws against producing and downloading child pornography, there are few other rules or laws regulating what can be seen or heard online.

Certainly, there are state and federal criminal statutes that prohibit use of the Internet to commit thefts. Nevertheless, people who use the Internet to buy merchandise must constantly be on guard against identity theft because thieves trawl the web looking for credit card numbers to exploit. Most people who have e-mail accounts have encountered suspicious pleas from phony foreign potentates asking for bank account numbers because they need a safe place to hide their riches. In reality, the con artists behind those e-mails hope to loot the bank accounts of people who foolishly provide the information.

What Is Censorware?

Because the government is largely unable to regulate Internet content, a number of private companies have stepped in, providing parents, schools, and libraries with what is known as "censorware" software. Among the titles available on the market are AOL Parental Controls, Net Nanny, Cyber Patrol, CYBERsitter, EyeGuard, Cyber Snoop, SurfWatch, and SmartFilter.

Censorware works by blocking access to websites that include certain keywords the program is directed to avoid. For example, by entering the keywords *blackjack* or *poker* into the censorware program, the computer user would be unable to access Internet gambling sites.

Despite the good intentions of censorware developers, the software does have its limitations. For example, the software could block keywords that have legitimate purposes. A student seeking information on breast cancer might be thwarted because *breast* may also be a keyword found on pornographic sites. Says Elisabeth Peelor, a student at Healdsburg High School in Sonoma County, California, "Censorware inhibits students who are doing legitimate research for school, it prevents teachers from accessing educational materials, and all in all it does more harm than good."

Moreover, totalitarian states such as China and Cuba have used censorware to block access to the Internet by their citizens—not out of a desire to protect young people from gambling or pornographic sites but to suppress civil rights.

Elisabeth Peelor, "Censorware: Doing More Harm than Good," *Santa Rosa (CA) Press-Democrat*, March 11, 2010. http://teenlife.blogs.pressdemocrat.com.

Meanwhile, though, many otherwise law-abiding people do not see anything wrong with using P2P software to share music without compensating the artists or other creative people involved in the production of the songs. The RIAA and other trade organizations treat the issue very seriously and have aggressively pursued cases against file-sharing websites, providers of P2P software, and even the downloaders. Indeed, Tenenbaum is not alone—many other music downloaders have also been sued by the RIAA, which usually wins the cases. In 2009, for example, Jammie Thomas-Rasset, a mother of four who lives in Minnesota, was found to have illegally downloaded 24 songs with Kazaa software and ordered to pay a whopping $1.9 million in damages. Later, a judge reduced the damages to $54,000. Still, Thomas-Rasset says she cannot afford the judgment. "It's not like I have a money tree in the backyard,"[54] she says.

The judgments against downloaders like Tenenbaum and Thomas-Rasset are extremely high because the RIAA contends that when they obtained file-sharing software, they made songs available on their computers to millions of other customers. Therefore, the RIAA says, they should be liable for the potential economic impact that downloading has on the record industry.

The Ugly Mugs Go Global

In the years following the creation of MP3 technology, the recording industry did not quite know what to make of this new way to listen to music. At the time, music on compact discs dominated the market: First introduced in the early 1980s, it had not taken long for CDs to drive vinyl albums, 8-track recordings, and cassette tapes into near extinction. The executives of the major recording labels did not regard MP3 files and the Internet as major threats against their empires. At the dawn of the MP3 age, it would have taken considerable foresight for anyone to see the enormous commercial potential of digitized music.

> "The music industry is acting like a digital police force."[53]
>
> —Charles Nesson, attorney for music downloader Joel Tenenbaum.

Most of the early stars of the digital music scene were amateur musicians like Jeff Patterson. When he was not studying computer science at the University of California at Santa Cruz, Patterson led a local garage band known as the Ugly Mugs. In 1993 Patterson and another computer science student, Rob Lord, digitized the music from Patterson's band and posted the songs on an Internet newsgroup site. Within days they discovered that the Ugly Mugs had a lot of fans in places like Turkey and Russia who were downloading the music and e-mailing pleas to Patterson and Lord to post more songs online.

Over the next few years, several websites were created that invited amateurs to post their music online for free distribution to anybody who owned a computer and a modem. Soon, more than just garage band music could be found online. Many fans were using their computers to lift tracks off CDs recorded by mainstream artists and posting those songs online as well. Even so, the recording industry still did not recognize the MP3 format as a threat to the music business. At this time, most Internet users were still using dial-up service while microprocessors were still not very powerful. Only an extremely dedicated music fan would be willing to wait 30 minutes or more to download a 2- or 3-minute song.

And so, in 1999, as record industry executives sat atop their empires, they ignored the many file-sharing websites that seemed to be popping up all over the web, including what was clearly emerging as the most popular of the sites. That website was known as Napster.

Napster Goes Live

Napster was started by 19-year-old college student Shawn Fanning, a self-taught computer programmer. When Fanning established Napster, there was already a lot of free music available on the Internet, but it was largely found on amateur websites. To locate a certain song, an Internet user had to make use of a search engine, like Yahoo or Google, and hope that the song would be available for downloading on somebody's website.

Fanning conceived Napster as a central site for music file-sharing. Users logged in and used a search feature to find the songs they desired. Napster then linked the member with another member who had digitized the song. Napster did not actually store the music on its servers, but it did facilitate the file sharing because the download commands had to go through Napster.

Napster went live in July 1999. By October of that year, 150,000 music fans had registered as users; they had access to more than 3 million songs. By July 2000 Napster had registered more than 20 million users.

Many of Napster's members were college students and other young people rebelling against the high prices the record companies charge for CDs—usually $16 or more for an album recorded by a top artist.

Moreover, the typical music buyer was usually only interested in one or two tracks on the CD but to get those songs was forced to buy the whole disc. During the vinyl age, record companies produced 45s—so named because they were played on turn-tables at the speed of 45 revolutions per minute. The 45s were small and inexpensive records that featured two songs, one on each side. Therefore, a fan did not have to buy the whole album to hear the song he or she really wanted to own. In the CD age, though, single-song CDs were rare, meaning fans were usually stuck shelling out a lot of cash for a lot of music they did not want. With the arrival of the MP3 format, it was now possible for a fan to obtain just the song he or she desired—and to get it for free.

> **"If you can afford a computer, you can afford to pay $16 for my CD."** [55]
>
> —Rapper Eminem.

As the number of songs available through Napster grew into the millions, the record companies finally took notice. Many of the world's top recording artists saw their royalties declining and reacted bitterly. "If you can afford a computer, you can afford to pay $16 for my CD,"[55] fumed rapper Eminem.

Napster Under Siege

Eminem was not the only artist who felt cheated by Napster. Rapper Dr. Dre sued Napster, claiming copyright infringement. So did the hard-rock band Metallica. The band's drummer, Lars Ulrich, was particularly vocal in his attacks on the website. He showed up at Napster headquarters in California and demanded that all of Metallica's songs be blocked from downloading through the website. "All I want is for artists who want to get paid to get paid,"[56] he declared.

Pop star Madonna also lost royalties due to Napster. In 2000 a pirated version of her single "Music" was made available through Napster—before it had been released to stores on CD. Evidently, somebody who worked for the recording studio obtained a version of the song and leaked it onto the Internet. "This music was stolen and was not intended for release for several months. It is still a work in progress," said Madonna's manager, Caresse Norman. "Those sites that offered a download of Madonna's music are violating her rights as an artist."[57]

The peer-to-peer file-sharing site Napster was a huge success, but it came under fire by musicians who were angry at the loss of royalties from sales. Napster founder Shawn Fanning (left) and the company's CEO, Hank Barry (right), appear at a 2001 news conference.

By now Napster was under siege, having been sued by several artists as well as record labels, charging that the website was costing them tens of millions of dollars in lost royalties. The courts ruled against Napster, finding that the website had provided users with a means to obtain music without compensating the people who produced it—a violation of copyright laws. Napster ceased operation as a P2P site on May 14, 2002, although it was later revived by the retailer Best Buy, which converted it into a legal music sales site.

Grokster, Morpheus, and Kazaa

Napster may have gone away as a P2P site, but file sharing still continues on the Internet. Following the demise of Napster as a file-sharing site, websites known as Grokster, Kazaa, and Morpheus were established. Instead of routing the file sharing through a central server, as Napster had done, Grokster and the others made software available that enabled file-sharers to connect directly with one another.

These sites insisted that they did not violate copyright laws, since they were merely making software available to users—how that software was used was beyond their control. In 2005 challenges against these sites were heard by the US Supreme Court, which ruled in favor of the recording companies, finding that they were being unfairly denied royalties through P2P software. As a result, Kazaa has converted into a legal music sales site, and Grokster and Morpheus have closed down.

But even the disappearance of these sites has not stopped the illegal commerce in music. One survey, conducted in 2008 by the University of Hertfordshire in Great Britain, concluded that the average teenager's digital music player stores no fewer than 800 illegally downloaded songs.

Meanwhile, with the arrival of faster Internet speeds and more powerful microprocessors in home computers, larger volumes of information can be downloaded in shorter periods of time. This technological advancement has led to widespread piracy of feature-length movies—an unthinkable notion in the era of dial-up Internet service. Following the strategy of the RIAA, in 2011 a movie industry association known as the US Copyright Group announced that it would pursue cases against individuals believed to be illegally downloading movies.

Shoplifting vs. Downloading

Copyright experts believe that otherwise law-abiding people download music and movies illegally because there is often not a clear distinction between what type of downloading is legal or illegal. They acknowledge that while it may be illegal to download free music through a P2P connection, it is not illegal to obtain the same song on a flash drive from a friend's laptop.

Moreover, not all content on the Internet is copyrighted—a lot of music and video is produced by amateurs. Some of it is of high quality, and in many cases it would appear there is little to distinguish such content from copyrighted works. Says British copyright law expert Rana Nader, "Downloading is so easy, and there is so much free content on the

Internet, it is hard to distinguish between illegal downloading, streaming free content and copying from a friend's laptop."[58]

Nader adds that many young people and others do not equate downloading with stealing. Many downloaders who would never think of walking into a store and stealing a CD have no qualms about downloading a song through a P2P connection. "When the product is digital, it does not feel like stealing,"[59] says Nader.

> "Downloading is so easy, and there is so much free content on the Internet, it is hard to distinguish between illegal downloading, streaming free content and copying from a friend's laptop."[58]
>
> —Copyright law expert Rana Nader.

A 2011 study by psychologists at the University of Nebraska confirmed that belief. The Nebraska psychologists surveyed 172 students who stated overwhelmingly that stealing a CD is morally wrong but downloading a song and not paying for it is a much less severe violation. According to psychology professor Talia Wingrove, who headed the study, students largely believe that it is not morally wrong to download music, and there is no societal pressure against downloading. Also, the study found they are ignorant of copyright laws that prohibit downloading, and even if they are aware of those laws they feel no obligation to obey them.

Offshore Gambling Sites

While authorities have found success in applying copyright laws to Internet content, they have been less successful in regulating access to sites that offer gambling over the web. In Nevada, New Jersey, and other states where casinos are located, 21 is usually the minimum age for admission. The minimum age for admission to an online gambling site is often lower—most usually demand proof that the player is at least 18. Even so, many younger players find ways to skirt the rules.

Oscar Santana, an eleventh-grade student at Edward R. Murrow High School in Brooklyn, New York, is a devotee of Texas hold 'em, a variation of poker. Santana plays Texas hold 'em online. He also gambles and boasts that he has been as much as $400 ahead in winnings. "I could spend a good two hours playing poker on the computer,"[60] says Santana.

The high school student is able to play because a college-age friend permits him to use his account at a poker website.

US lawmakers have been largely unable to regulate online gambling. Gambling websites are typically based offshore in places like Great Britain, Costa Rica, and Gibraltar, where the US legal system has no jurisdiction. Even when websites are legally registered in offshore locations, hundreds of miles from American jurisdiction, any Internet user can, of course, access them in seconds.

A game of Texas hold 'em brings out the serious competitors in Las Vegas. Online poker games also attract serious gamblers, but regulation is difficult because many of the websites that host these games operate in places that are not subject to US laws.

How Are Movies Pirated?

According to the Motion Picture Association of America, some 90 percent of movies downloaded from the web are made available by people who smuggle camcorders into theaters. After recording the movie, they upload it onto the Internet, making it available through illegal file-sharing sites.

This type of thievery has had a significant impact on the film industry. Barry Meyer, chief executive officer of the movie studio Warner Brothers, says theft of movies over the Internet costs the Hollywood film industry as much as $20 billion a year.

A typical example could be found in the losses suffered by the 2009 film *Sherlock Holmes*, which starred Robert Downey Jr. The movie earned more than $200 million in receipts at the box office, but Meyer says the film was illegally downloaded nearly 1.8 million times within 30 days of its premiere in theaters. If the movie had not been downloaded, and all 1.8 million of those viewers had bought tickets—at an average cost of $7.50—*Sherlock Holmes* would have earned at least another $13.5 million at the box office.

Young People Listen to Their Parents

Because there is a lack of governmental regulation over what can be accessed on the Internet, child safety advocates urge young people to talk with their parents about what is acceptable content. Surveys do indicate that when it comes to using the Internet, young people listen to their parents. A 2010 study by the Kaiser Family Foundation of Menlo Park, California, found that young people whose parents counsel them on proper Internet use spend three hours less online each day than young people who receive no guidance from their parents. "The reality is that teenagers care deeply about what their parents think,"[61] says Philadelphia pediatrician Kenneth Ginsburg.

Moreover, advocacy groups such as the Family Online Safety Institute and Website Rating and Advisory Council have provided tips on responsible Internet use. The Website Rating and Advisory Council also provides free content-control software, known as the Parent Control Bar, that blocks pornographic sites, gambling sites, and similar sources of content. A number of for-profit companies also make content-control software, also known as "censorware," available to consumers.

Lawlessness and the Internet

US lawmakers have been hesitant to regulate content on the Internet—finding that to do so would violate the principles of free speech on which democracies are based. That is why pornography is so widely available on the Internet—as Congress learned in the Communications Decency Act case, restrictions that would regulate access to online pornography could also be applied to political speech. Such laws are unconstitutional.

Meanwhile, state legislatures have for many years applied regulations on state lotteries, casinos, horse racing tracks, and other forms of gambling—even bingo parlors—but because Internet gambling sites are located offshore, they have been beyond the reach of lawmakers.

As for regulating file sharing, American courts rely on copyright laws to ensure writers, artists, music producers, and filmmakers are not cheated out of the royalties they deserve. However, given the lawless nature of the Internet—and the fact that most people see nothing wrong with downloading free music and movies—it does not appear likely that the Internet will shed its Wild West image any time soon.

Chapter Five

What Is the Future of Online Entertainment?

The 2010 MTV Video Music Awards broadcast did more than provide fans with a glimpse of Katy Perry's barely there gown, Ke$ha's black micromini fashioned out of a garbage bag, and will.i.am's UFO-inspired techno-goggles and pulsating clamshell skullcap. As these stars and others strutted in front of their fans, two 28-foot-high (8.5m) screens perched on the stage displayed the ongoing comments from viewers sending out Twitter messages from home.

As such, the awards show marked something of a milestone in the long history of television broadcasting: TV had finally become interactive. Instead of just sitting at home watching images and hearing sounds, fans could now talk back to the TV—communicating in real time with the people they were viewing on their screens. For example, Lady Gaga did not have to wait until the next morning to read the newspapers to find out what her critics thought of her outrageous dress sewn together from slabs of red meat. All she had to do was check her smartphone or even glance at the screens atop the stage, which were displaying some of the 9,200 tweets a minute transmitted by the show's viewers.

As TV and the Internet move into the future, viewers can expect to have many more opportunities to interact with live programming—and not just by sending out tweets. TV executives are exploring ways in which they can merge the interactive qualities of the Internet with TV broadcasting, giving viewers more opportunities to be participants in content instead of merely passive viewers. "This is about democratizing a

Lady Gaga showed up at the 2010 MTV Video Music Awards wearing a dress made from slabs of meat. Viewers reacted to the singer's outrageous costume by sending 9,200 tweets a minute, many of which were displayed on-screen during the show.

one-to-many medium, giving people a voice in the creation and distribution of content,"[62] says former US vice president Al Gore, a founder of the network Current TV.

Fact-Checking from Home

Current TV first merged Twitter commentary into programming in 2008 when producers selected tweets from viewers to stream across the bottom of the screen during the presidential debates. Current TV called the project Hack the Debate. As the candidates debated health care, for example, the producers streamed viewer tweets such as, "This discussion about universal health care makes me want to pop some pills!"[63] The tweets provided more than just humorous commentary—some viewers at home tweeted facts and figures to point out how the candidates often strayed from the truth while making their arguments. As a result, the tweeting viewers served as home-based fact checkers.

These tweets were not truly interactive—the candidates could not read the comments sent from viewers during the debates—nevertheless, Current TV had shown how the Internet could give voice to viewers as they watched a news-making event unfold on their screens.

Interactive TV has been a dream of network executives for decades, dating back well before the Internet era. In the 1950s the animated children's program *Winky Dink and You* established itself as the first—and only—interactive TV show when it invited young fans to draw on their screens to complete the action in the story. The children did not *actually* draw on their TV screens—parents placed clear vinyl sheets across the screens; afterward, the crayon pictures could be wiped clean.

Winky Dink and You may have been decidedly low-tech, but the show did give children an opportunity to be more than just passive viewers. For the next several years, though, efforts to make TV interactive were largely unsuccessful. Proponents of interactive TV were mainly held back by the limits of the technology: TV was simply just a one-way medium.

"This is about democratizing a one-to-many medium, giving people a voice in the creation and distribution of content."[62]

—Former US vice president Al Gore, a founder of Current TV.

The Future of Avatars

Online game players often attempt to make their avatars resemble themselves. To help gamers, several companies provide online services that help people make their avatars look like the gamers they represent. One company, Mego, uses images produced by a webcam that provides a mirror image of the player on the screen. Julia Johnston, founder of Mego, says female players are much more interested in projecting images of themselves than are male players, who tend to fictionalize their images. "The majority of our users are, of course, in the 14-to-17 range and are primarily girls," she says.

The use of online avatars is expected to grow. Many companies see advertising opportunities and are making virtual products available to avatars, hoping to get their brand names and logos into the online gaming environments. "Brands want to build loyalty and aspiration in these kinds of young consumers," says Las Vegas, Nevada, marketing consultant Diane Nelson Koznick. "A 14-year-old could never buy a $10,000 Valentino gown or the hot new Marc Jacobs bag. But she can buy the $5 version for her avatar. Once you pay money, you have a sense of ownership and identification with that brand."

Quoted in Leanne Delap, "Realistic Avatars Get All Dressed Up," *Toronto Star*, January 6, 2011, p. L1.

The Picturephone

Still, in 1964 Bell Telephone Laboratories provided a brief glimpse into the future when it debuted an innovation at the New York World's Fair: the Picturephone. It was an attempt to merge TV with the telephone. The desktop contraption included a tiny camera and TV screen, enabling callers not only to speak with one another but to see each other as well.

The device made quite a splash at the World's Fair. To use the phone, visitors were invited to step into a booth and speak with someone on another Picturephone stationed cross-country at Disneyland in California. Later, Bell advertised the Picturephone as "crossing a telephone with a TV set."[64]

But the Picturephone never caught on—the picture quality was poor, the price for the service was prohibitively expensive, and Bell Telephone's market research indicated most people felt uncomfortable with the notion of being seen during a telephone conversation. Bell Telephone soon scuttled the Picturephone, but nearly 40 years after the device made its brief debut on the market, Swedish entrepreneurs introduced Skype—enabling people to talk and, through the use of webcams, see one another over Internet connections. By 2010 some 600 million Internet users had installed Skype on their computers.

QUBE and the Full Service Network

The next attempt to make TV interactive occurred in 1977 with the introduction of TV programming known as QUBE. It was actually a cable TV package that offered 30 channels to subscribers, including 10 channels that purported to be interactive. QUBE subscribers received set-top boxes featuring controls they could use to interact with the broadcast content. They could, for example, participate in game shows and respond to polls. During a presidential speech, QUBE subscribers could cast votes on whether they agreed with what the president was saying; the results were tallied and displayed on the screen during the telecast. There was also original QUBE programming, such as talent shows, that gave viewers at home the opportunity to vote for contestants. However, the QUBE programming was expensive to produce and never made a profit. In 1984 QUBE went quietly off the air.

Telecommunications companies spent the next two decades trying to improve on the QUBE concept, but their efforts largely proved to be failures. In 1995, for example, the media company Time Warner attempted to develop the Full Service Network (FSN). It was an ambitious project that would enable viewers to use their TVs to order music and video on demand, scan the news, place classified advertisements,

> "Increasingly, our customer base multitasks. While they watch television, they may be online researching that show, or in the case of reality programming voting or actually participating in the show in some way."[66]
>
> —David Purdy, vice president of Canadian telecommunications company Rogers Communications.

play games, access educational content, buy tickets to sporting and entertainment events, browse library collections, and even check their bank accounts. Time Warner tested FSN by providing the network to 4,000 homes in Orlando, Florida. After two years, though, Time Warner closed down the project, suffering a loss of $100 million.

FSN failed because of the vast technical issues involved in making TV interactive without the Internet. FSN employed telephone lines and TV cable to transmit the signals—meaning they had to compete with voice communications and TV broadcasts for space in the lines. Also, the set-top controllers required for network communications cost about $1,000—a price most homeowners were unwilling to pay.

Still, even as Time Warner pulled the plug on FSN, many entertainment executives knew that interactive TV was inevitable. They suspected that the Internet would provide the technological means to make it happen. Wrote a *Time* magazine journalist in 1996, "That heady moment is approaching when home computers linked to a more TV-like web will emerge as a lucrative entertainment medium in their own right."[65]

Personal Video Recording

It would take another decade for network speeds to improve and microprocessors to achieve enough power so that TV producers could begin to make their content interactive. And given the limited ability people at home still have in becoming active participants in TV programming, it could be argued that there is still a lot of interactivity ahead.

There is no question that TV producers see interactivity as a way to revive a mode of entertainment that has been on the wane. In 1979 the three top-rated shows on network TV were *Three's Company*, *M*A*S*H*, and *That's Incredible*. Each boasted a weekly rating of 21, meaning that while those shows were on the air, at least 21 percent of the viewing public was watching. In 2009 the top-rated shows on network TV were *NCIS* and *Sunday Night Football*—each scored a rating of 13. In other words, fewer people are watching TV because more people are spending time on the Internet. To get people back to watching TV, network executives hope to make the Internet a more integral part of the TV experience.

While watching TV, viewers will be able to use the screen for a number of purposes: not only to watch content, but to check their e-mail, shop online, send out tweets, and even order pizza to be delivered—before the movie ends. "If you look at our entertainment experiences, they used to be very passive, where we'd lean back and just take it all in," says David Purdy, vice president of Rogers Communications, a Canadian-based telecommunications company. "Increasingly, our customer base multitasks. While they watch television, they may be online researching that show, or in the case of reality programming voting or actually participating in the show in some way."[66]

Some experts are predicting the arrival of what is known as "personalized TV." By hooking their computers to their TV sets, viewers will be able to time shift the programs—making them available at times most convenient to the viewers. Time shifting can already be accomplished through TiVo and similar services, but using the Internet to create personalized TV viewing will enable viewers to do much more. They can pause, rewind, or fast forward the programs. The content can also be displayed in slow motion or freeze frame. Moreover, by entering keywords in an Internet link, viewers can program their televisions to search broadcast networks for specific titles, time slots, actors, themes, parental ratings, and other criteria. "Hence, a personal video recorder generally makes it possible for the viewers to see what they want, when they want it,"[67] says Jens F. Jensen, a Danish economist and an expert on interactive TV.

> **"People want to watch sports live if they can, wherever they are."[69]**
>
> —Damon Phillips, vice president of ESPN3.

Creating Their Own Channels

Personalized video recording is the first step toward enabling TV viewers to essentially create their own channels, pulling together the type of programming they want to see from the Internet. Once the viewer creates a record of what he or she seeks on the Internet, software will intuitively search for that type of content and integrate it into the viewer's programming schedule.

One service that has taken a step toward enabling viewers to create their own channels is Ffwd—shorthand for "fast forward." "In Ffwd, you can subscribe to or create a channel for any interest you have and get related content," says Ffwd founder Patrick Koppula. "Once a user sub-

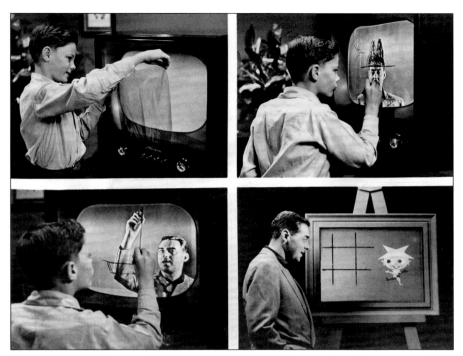

The 1950s children's television program Winky Dink and You *was the first interactive program on television. As instructed by the show's host, a young boy draws on a vinyl sheet placed on his television set. Efforts to make TV interactive are ongoing.*

scribes to about seven channels, Ffwd takes that information and . . . creates a personalized channel. The system makes intuitive decisions to your programming stream."[68]

Sports programming is expected to be most in demand as people create their own TV channels, employing the Internet to follow their favorite teams or athletes. Indeed, as services like Ffwd start trawling through the web for programming, they may find a lot of what their viewers seek on ESPN3.

Owned by the sports cable network ESPN, ESPN3 is a website that enables fans to stream live athletic events on their home computers. This service has proved to be particularly popular with people who live far from home—such as college students and military personnel—who cannot find broadcasts of their favorite teams on local TV stations. "People want to watch sports live if they can, wherever they are," says Damon

Phillips, vice president of ESPN3. "Around this company, we talk about the 'best available screen.' If a fan can't watch what he wants on his 52-inch flat panel, [ESPN3] is there. It's a full-fledged TV network that just happens to be delivered through the Internet."[69] According to Phillips, ESPN3 streams some 40 live events each day. Moreover, viewers can stream up to 14 events simultaneously.

A significant portion of viewers who access ESPN3 are people from other countries who live in the United States. These viewers can find few broadcasts on American TV of the sports they love, such as rugby and cricket as well as European soccer and basketball leagues.

Another type of programming that might be found on personalized channels is canceled TV series. While they aired, these series may have generated a dedicated following among fans. Now that these shows are off the air, the shows' producers can make the old episodes available on the Internet so that fans can continue to enjoy them.

Smart TV

While some programmers look for ways to make broadcast TV content available on the Internet, others are finding ways to make Internet content available on the TV. In the near future, experts believe it will be common for people to connect their laptops to their 60-inch (152cm) plasma TV sets, giving them a high-def experience while surfing the web.

TV owners can already make these connections, but it takes some extra hardware as well as a degree of expertise. TV manufacturers have already started producing what are known as Smart TVs, otherwise known as Connected TVs, that will provide dedicated ports for laptop connections. "Increasingly, your television is being connected to the web, and with that you end up with a very different experience of finding and consuming content,"[70] says Edward Williams, a financial analyst who follows the entertainment industry.

Ramping Up Bandwidth

In addition to TV sets, gaming consoles are also being integrated into the mix: Instead of just serving as platforms for games, the consoles will also deliver movies and Internet content. Mark Kroese, general manager

Google TV

Google, the company that provides Internet users with a hugely popular search engine, plans to make a big impact as a provider of content for Smart TV. In 2010 the company launched Google TV—a project to make the television set the primary device in the home for accessing the web. At first, the company plans to provide a set-top device that will connect the TV to the Internet, but Google is also working with the Japanese electronics company Sony to design TV sets in which the Internet-connecting hardware will be engineered right into the TV. Another component of Google TV will be a wireless keyboard, enabling TV watchers to type in website addresses and watch as the images on their TV screens jump to those sites.

Given Google's popularity as a search engine—68 percent of all Internet searches, or some 2.4 billion searches a day, are conducted through the Google search bar—entertainment industry insiders are following the development of Google TV. Industry watchers suggest that if any company can merge TV with the Internet, it will be Google. Says Paul Gagnon, an analyst with the market research firm Display Search, "The question becomes is [web browsing] something people really want to do on their TV, or are they content to use their laptops?"

Quoted in Mike Freeman, "Sony Teams Up with Google on Internet TV," *San Diego Union-Tribune*, October 13, 2010.

for entertainment devices at Microsoft, envisions the company's Xbox as a "very all-purpose media consumption device in the living room for 100 million, 200 million people."[71] Meanwhile, the manufacturers of the Wii, Xbox, and PlayStation have entered into agreements with the DVD rental service Netflix to provide movies over their game consoles. These movies will be streamed through Internet connections.

All of these advancements will continue to develop as engineers deliver higher degrees of bandwidth. As the network administrators continue to ramp up bandwidth, the quality of the content is expected to improve as well. Indeed, while today the Internet is a combination of text, graphics, still photos, and video, with more bandwidth video may come to dominate Internet content. John Chambers, the chief executive officer of Cisco Systems, which designs and produces networking technology, has predicted that in the future, 90 percent of Internet content will be video. "The video experience was not really ready for the big time until now,"[72] he says.

With access to more bandwidth, TV and game producers are expected to deliver content with improved, high-definition graphics as well as 3-D imagery. Three-dimensional play has been available in gaming for more than a decade. It has received mixed reviews from players, some of whom find it enticing while others find the 3-D graphics confusing and difficult to maneuver through. As 3-D imaging improves, though, many gamers are looking forward to entering a *World of Warcraft* universe where the action can come from almost any angle. "I have a sense that [TV viewers] haven't had an opportunity to really explore the truly transmedia experiences offered by broadband Internet and its connection to TV," says Gary Carter, chief operating officer of FremantleMedia, an entertainment production company. "We need to see if innovative people and companies can make these things real."[73]

Improvements in technology mean games, videos, and other Internet content will not just be found on home computers or plasma TVs fixed to family room walls. The Internet has already made the transition to mobile devices such as tablets and smartphones; these devices will clearly become more common in the future. Meanwhile, as wireless networks expand, there will be more places where people can find access to the Internet away from home. Now, people can pick up wireless network signals, known as Wi-Fi, in many places—among them public libraries, college campuses, and hotels, but also some public parks, coffee bars, and sidewalk cafes.

Many communities have announced ambitious plans to provide citywide Wi-Fi. And in 2010 Singapore Airlines said it would outfit its airplanes to provide wireless networks to passengers on transpacific flights—meaning that even at 50,000 feet (15,240m), people will be able

> "The video experience was not really ready for the big time until now."[72]
>
> —John Chambers, chief executive officer of Cisco Systems.

to use their laptops, tablets, or phones to watch movies, play games, or tweet about Lady Gaga's peculiar taste in fashion as they explore the vast entertainment potential of the Internet.

The Internet Has Always Been Entertaining

In the earliest days of the Internet, it would have taken a considerable amount of foresight to see the potential of entertainment transmitted through cyberspace. Those early days of the Internet featured slow modem speeds, weak processing capabilities, and a lack of content. And yet the Internet has always been an entertaining place. The first users of the Internet were delighted to be able to place *Spacewar!*, and it is likely that many of them played for hours at a time. Those first videos posted online may have taken a half hour or more to download, and yet people endured frozen screens and many idle minutes anticipating the hoped-for content.

> "I have a sense that [TV viewers] haven't had an opportunity to really explore the truly trans-media experiences offered by broadband Internet and its connection to TV. We need to see if innovative people and companies can make these things real."[73]
>
> —Gary Carter, chief operating officer of FremantleMedia.

The first YouTube video, *Me at the Zoo*, ran for a mere 18 seconds and shows nothing more than Jawed Karim commenting on the length of an elephant's trunk, and yet many people have appreciated the brief video for its entertainment value. By early 2011 *Me at the Zoo* was still available on YouTube and, in the 6 years since its debut, had been viewed by more than 4.6 million people.

Interactive TV, better 3-D imaging, and more mobile access to the Internet are all part of the future of cyberspace. Clearly, the Internet will be a big part of the entertainment world in the years to come.

Source Notes

Introduction: A Vast Source of Entertainment

1. Quoted in Matt Richtel, "Growing Up Digital," *Junior Scholastic*, February 28, 2011, p. 6.
2. Aaron Smith, "The Internet as a Diversion," Pew Internet & American Life Project, September 10, 2009. www.pewinternet.org.
3. Quoted in Richtel, "Growing Up Digital," p. 6.
4. Recording Industry Association of America, "For Students Doing Reports," 2011. www.riaa.com.

Chapter One: How the Internet Dominates the Entertainment World

5. Quoted in David Kushner, "The Baby Billionaires of Silicon Valley," *Rolling Stone*, November 16, 2006, p. 60.
6. Quoted in Dave Itzkoff, "Nerds in the Hood, Stars on the Web," *New York Times*, December 27, 2005, p. E1.
7. Pew Internet & American Life Project, "Online Video Proliferates as Viewers Share What They Find Online," July 25, 2007. www.pewinternet.org.
8. Chris O'Malley, "Drowning in the Net," *Popular Science*, June 1995, pp. 84–85.
9. Matt Barton, *Dungeons and Desktops: The History of Computer Role-Playing Games*. Wellesley, MA: AK Peters, 2008, p. 25.
10. Barton, *Dungeons and Desktops*, p. 26.
11. Marty Toohey, "*World of Warcraft* Blurs the Line Between the Real and the Virtual—Maybe Too Much," *Austin (TX) American-Statesman*, March 29, 2008, p. F7.
12. Quoted in Steve Knopper, *Appetite for Self-Destruction: The Spectacular Crash of the Record Industry in the Digital Age*. New York: Free Press, 2009, p. 117.
13. Quoted in CBS News, "Apple Marks 10 Billionth Song Download," February 26, 2010. www.cbsnews.com.

Chapter Two: Does Online Gaming Isolate Players?

14. Quoted in Alison Smith-Squire, "Happy Ever Avatar! Married, the Couple Who Fell in Love in Online Game Before They'd Ever Met," *Daily Mail* (London), November 13, 2010, p. 3.

15. Arnold Brown, "Relations, Community and Identity in the New Virtual Society," *Futurist*, March–April 2011, p. 29.

16. comScore, "Worldwide Online Gaming Community Reaches 217 Million People," July 10, 2007. www.comscore.com.

17. Quoted in Cynthia Reynolds, "Videogame Widows," *Maclean's*, January 16, 2006, p. 42.

18. *Hardware*, "*Star Wars Galaxies*: The Jar Jar of MMORP Games?," August 2003, p. 90.

19. Barton, *Dungeons and Desktops*, p. 200.

20. Quoted in Reynolds, "Videogame Widows," p. 42.

21. Quoted in Steve Mollman, "For Online Addicts, Relationships Float Between Real, Virtual Worlds," CNN, January 29, 2008. http://edition.cnn.com.

22. Quoted in Mollman, "For Online Addicts, Relationships Float Between Real, Virtual Worlds."

23. Quoted in Mollman, "For Online Addicts, Relationships Float Between Real, Virtual Worlds."

24. Quoted in Corinne Lestch, "Video Games Might Aid Depression," *Daily Northwestern*, February 19, 2009. www.dailynorthwestern.com.

25. Quoted in David Kohn, "Addicted: Suicide over EverQuest?," CBS News, October 18, 2002. www.cbsnews.com.

26. Quoted in Fox News, "Chinese *Warcraft* Game Distributor Sued over Teen's Suicide," May 12, 2006. www.foxnews.com.

27. Quoted in Xinhua News Agency, "Parents Sue Online Game Seller for Son's Suicide," May 12, 2006. www.china.org.cn.

28. Henry Jenkins, "Reality Bytes: Eight Myths About Video Games Debunked," *The Video Game Revolution*, PBS, 2004. www.pbs.org.

29. Quoted in *Discover*, "Games Without Frontiers," September 2010, p. 66.

30. Quoted in *Discover*, "Games Without Frontiers," p. 66.

31. Quoted in Lestch, "Video Games Might Aid Depression."
32. Quoted in *The Fifth Estate*, "Strangers in Paradise: The Gamer Widow," CBC, January 28, 2009. www.cbc.ca.
33. Quoted in *The Fifth Estate*, "Strangers in Paradise."

Chapter Three: Can Online Entertainment Be Addictive?

34. Quoted in Mattathias Schwartz, "The Hold-'Em Holdup," *New York Times Magazine*, June 11, 2006, p. E52.
35. Quoted in Elisabeth Deffner, "Gambling Away Your Future," *Listen*, October 2009, p. 7.
36. Quoted in Schwartz, "The Hold-'Em Holdup," p. E52.
37. Quoted in Schwartz, "The Hold-'Em Holdup," p. E52.
38. Quoted in Schwartz, "The Hold-'Em Holdup," p. E52.
39. Quoted in ABC News, "Online Gambling: A Growing Addiction," January 1, 2006. http://abcnews.go.com.
40. Quoted in ABC News, "Online Gambling."
41. Quoted in Matthew Moore, "*World of Warcraft*: Teenager Collapses After 24-Hour Gaming Session," *Daily Telegraph* (London), November 18, 2008. www.telegraph.co.uk.
42. Quoted in Simon Husted, "Students Pick Video Games over Social Life," KentWired.com, January 21, 2010. http://kentwired.com.
43. Quoted in Jennifer Crossley, "Wired: Internet Addiction Center Growing Quickly," *Florence (AL) Times Daily*, October 4, 2009. www.timesdaily.com.
44. Kimberly Young, "Some Interesting Statistics on Internet Addiction," Center for Internet Addiction Recovery, October 20, 2010. http://netaddictionrecovery.blogspot.com.
45. Quoted in Ellen Seidman, "My Husband Is Addicted to Internet Porn," *Ladies' Home Journal*, October 2010. www.lhj.com.
46. Hal Arkowitz and Scott O. Lilienfeld, "Sex in Bits and Bytes," *Scientific American Mind*, July/August 2010, p. 64.
47. Quoted in *Playboy*, "*Playboy* Interview: John Mayer," March 2010. www.playboy.com.
48. Quoted in *Current Events*, "Caught in the Web," September 28, 2009, p. 4.
49. Quoted in *Current Events*, "Caught in the Web," p. 4.

50. Quoted in Crossley, "Wired."

Chapter Four: Can Online Entertainment Be Regulated?

51. Quoted in *Toronto Star*, "File Sharer Did 'What Kids Do,'" July 29, 2009, p. E2.
52. Recording Industry Association of America, "About Music Copyright Notices," 2011. www.riaa.com.
53. Quoted in Nazanin Lankarini, "Push in Law Schools to Reform Copyright Laws; File-Sharing Crackdown Focuses on Students and Could Cost One $675,000," *International Herald-Tribune*, December 2, 2009.
54. Quoted in Raju Mudhar, "Damages Cut in Song-Sharing Case," *Toronto Star*, January 26, 2010, p. E2.
55. Quoted in Knopper, *Appetite for Self-Destruction*, p. 134.
56. Quoted in Knopper, *Appetite for Self-Destruction*, p. 135.
57. Quoted in John Borland, "Unreleased Madonna Single Slips onto Net," CNET News, June 1, 2000. http://news.cnet.com.
58. Quoted in Lankarini, "Push in Law Schools to Reform Copyright Laws; File-Sharing Crackdown Focuses on Students and Could Cost One $675,000."
59. Quoted in Lankarini, "Push in Law Schools to Reform Copyright Laws; File-Sharing Crackdown Focuses on Students and Could Cost One $675,000."
60. Quoted in Heidi Evans, "Experts: TV and Tournaments Are Raising Ante for Teens Playing Poker Online," *New York Daily News*, May 26, 2005.
61. Quoted in Kim Painter, "Teenagers Do Listen," *USA Today*, February 8, 2010, p. 6D.

Chapter Five: What Is the Future of Online Entertainment?

62. Quoted in Ellen McGirt, Tina Dupuy, and Danielle Sacks, "I Want My Twitter TV!," *Fast Company*, December 2010–January 2011, p. 98.
63. Quoted in McGirt, Dupuy, and Sacks, "I Want My Twitter TV!," p. 98.

64. Quoted in Jens F. Jensen, "Interactive Television—a Brief Media History," *Lecture Notes in Computer Science*, 2008, p. 3.
65. Michael Krantz, "Hollywood Gets Wired," *Time*, December 23, 1996. www.time.com.
66. Quoted in Carmi Levy, "Future of Television Is Online and On-Demand," *Toronto Star*, October 15, 2010. www.thestar.com.
67. Jensen, "Interactive Television—a Brief Media History," p. 8.
68. Quoted in Bill Barol, "Double Vision," *Fast Company*, February 2009, p. 17.
69. Quoted in Barol, "Double Vision," p. 17.
70. Quoted in Levy, "Future of Television Is Online and On-Demand."
71. Quoted in Brian Steinberg, "The Future of TV," *Advertising Age*, November 30, 2009, p. 1.
72. Quoted in Doug Olenick, "Cisco's Chambers Sees Video-Centric Web," *Week in Consumer Electronics*, January 18, 2010, p. 31.
73. Quoted in *Times of India*, "3D, Smart Devices Move Towards New Entertainment Era," March 31, 2011. http://timesofindia.indiatimes.com.

Facts About Online Gaming and Entertainment

- Blizzard Entertainment, the developer of *World of Warcraft*, announced in 2010 that more than 12 million people worldwide had registered to play the game.

- The Nielsen Company, which tracks entertainment trends, reported in January 2011 that Internet users spend 4 hours and 39 minutes a month watching online videos—a 45 percent increase over the time they devoted to online videos in January 2010.

- One year after its debut in 2005, YouTube was bought by Google for $1.6 billion. However, YouTube, which streams advertisements, did not make a profit until 2010.

- The Pew Internet & American Life Project reported in 2009 that 36 percent of all teenagers and young children watch a video on the Internet at least once a day; overall, Pew said, at least 19 percent of all Internet users watch a video at least once a day.

- The *Journal of Communications* reported the results of a 2010 study of 7,000 online gamers, finding that female players outnumber male players. The study said most women play to meet people online rather than for the competitive aspects of the game, which motivates most male players.

- A Brigham Young University study reported in 2011 that 12 percent of all websites are devoted to pornographic content and that 68 million people a day use Google and other search engines to find pornography on the web.

- The Nielsen Company reported in 2008 that 25 percent of American employees who have access to computers at work visit pornographic websites while on the job.

- A Chinese study reported by *Time* magazine in 2010 found that teenage online gamers are 2.5 times more likely to suffer depression than teenagers who do not play online games.

- A 2010 study by Nottingham Trent University in Great Britain reported that some of the common traits found in online gaming addicts are aggression, lack of self-control, a desire to seek new sensations, and anxiety.

- The Recording Industry Association of America reported in 2011 that 17 percent of the bandwidth available to American Internet users is devoted to downloading pornographic movies, streaming pirated versions of popular films, and downloading illegal copies of songs.

- By 2009 the Recording Industry Association of America had filed lawsuits against more than 18,000 Internet users, accusing them of illegally downloading songs. The average penalty paid by the defendants is $4,000.

- Producers of the Academy Award–winning film *The Hurt Locker* announced in 2010 they intend to sue at least 5,000 Internet users who have illegally downloaded the film.

- A 2008 study by the University of Hertfordshire in Great Britain reported that 89 percent of teens between the ages of 14 and 17 have obtained illegal copies of music; for people 18 to 24, the rate rises to 96 percent.

- Between 1999 and 2009, the Recording Industry Association of America reports, legal sales of music dropped from $14.6 billion a year to $7.7 billion a year. The association names illegal downloads as the reason for the drop in sales.

- Google reported in 2011 that YouTube is the second-most popular website on the Internet, receiving 85 million page views a day. (First is Facebook with 770 million.) Twelfth on the list is Youku—a Chinese version of YouTube—with 3.7 million page views.

- MTV's decision to air live tweets during the 2010 Video Music Awards telecast helped boost the audience to more than 11 million fans, a 27 percent increase over the previous year's audience.

- According to the electronics company Sony, engineering a 46-inch (117cm) plasma television set so that it can access Google TV is expected to raise the price of the set from $1,000 to $1,400.

- By 2010, 10 percent of the 2.9 million customers of Canadian tele-communications company Rogers Communications had signed up to access online content through their TV service.

- According to the Nielsen Company, by 2009 more than 17 million Americans were using their smartphones to view Internet content, a 60 percent increase over the number reported in 2008.

Related Organizations

American Gaming Association (AGA)

1299 Pennsylvania Ave. NW
Washington, DC 20004
phone: (202) 552-2675
website: www.americangaming.org

The AGA is the trade association representing the American casino industry. The AGA advocates for government regulation of online gambling to stamp out abuses in the industry, such as permitting play by underage gamblers. By accessing the link for "Fact Sheets," visitors to the website can find many statistics on Internet gambling.

Center for Internet Addiction Recovery

PO Box 72
Bradford, PA 16701
phone: (814) 451-2405
fax: (814) 368-9560
website: http://netaddiction.com

The treatment center for Internet addicts provides many resources for students seeking information on addiction to online gambling, gaming, and pornography. Visitors to the center's website can find a list of symptoms often displayed by Internet addicts as well as a blog on addiction written by Kimberly Young, the center's director.

Family Online Safety Institute (FOSI)

624 Ninth St. NW, Suite 222
Washington, DC 20001
website: www.fosi.org

The FOSI promotes responsible Internet use by young people and adults, providing tips on how to avoid Internet pornography, gambling sites, and other websites that could become addictive. Visitors to the FOSI website can download copies of the publication *Broadband Responsibility: A Blueprint for Safe and Responsible Online Use.*

Federal Communications Commission (FCC)

445 Twelfth St. SW
Washington, DC 20554
phone: (888) 225-5322
fax: (866) 418-0232
e-mail: fccinfo@fcc.gov
website: www.broadband.gov

Although the FCC provides little regulation over the content found on the Internet, the agency is involved in issues that affect Internet use. Visitors to the FCC website can read about the national plan to improve broadband service, making fast Internet speeds available to all Americans.

Motion Picture Association of America (MPAA)

1600 Eye St. NW
Washington, DC 20006
phone: (202) 293-1966
fax: (202) 296-7410
e-mail: contactus@mpaa.org
website: www.mpaa.org

The MPAA has launched a campaign to stem the availability of pirated movies online. Visitors to the MPAA website can learn about movie piracy by following the link to "Content Protection." Visitors can also follow a link to a related site, respectcopyrights.org, which provides tips on how to recognize pirated films online.

On-Line Gamers Anonymous (OLGA)

104 Miller Lane
Harrisburg, PA 17110
phone: (612) 245-1115
website: www.olganon.org

Founded by Elizabeth Woolley, whose son Shawn committed suicide while playing an MMORP game, OLGA provides support for people recovering from addictions to online gaming. Visitors to the OLGA website can find a chat room, bulletin boards, and other resources for helping people overcome their gaming addictions.

Pew Internet & American Life Project

1615 L St. NW, Suite 700
Washington, DC 20036
phone: (202) 419-4500
fax: (202) 419-4505
e-mail: info@pewinternet.org
website: http://pewinternet.org

The Pew Internet & American Life Project studies the use of the Internet by Americans. Visitors to the Pew website can find many studies about online entertainment, including *The State of Music Online: Ten Years After Napster*, *The State of Online Video*, and *The Internet as a Diversion*.

Recording Industry Association of America (RIAA)

1025 F St. NW, 10th Floor
Washington, DC 20004
phone: (202) 775-0101
website: www.riaa.com

The RIAA is the main trade association for recording industry professionals. The RIAA vigorously pursues piracy of copyrighted music, filing lawsuits against downloaders as well as websites that sell P2P software. Visitors can find many resources about music piracy on the RIAA website, including a link titled "For Students Doing Reports."

US Copyright Office

101 Independence Ave. SE
Washington, DC 20559-6000
phone: (202) 707-3000
website: www.copyright.gov

Music publishers, recording studios, filmmakers, and other creative people obtain copyright protection for intellectual content by registering their work with the US Copyright Office. Visitors to the agency's website can learn about copyright law by downloading the publications *Copyright Basics* and *Taking the Mystery Out of Copyright*.

Website Rating and Advisory Council (WRAAC)
930 Washington Ave., 3rd Floor
Miami Beach, FL 33139
phone: (305) 531-2979
e-mail: support@wraac.org
website: www.wraac.org

The WRAAC provides free software to parents who want to maintain control over the Internet content viewed by their children. Visitors to the WRAAC website can download the "Parental Control Bar," which provides filters that can block pornographic websites, gambling sites, and similar Internet venues.

For Further Research

Books

Nathan Fisk, *Understanding Online Piracy: The Truth About Illegal File Sharing*. Santa Barbara, CA: ABC-CLIO, 2009.

Ethan Gilsdorf, *Fantasy Freaks and Gaming Geeks: An Epic Quest for Reality Among Role Players, Online Gamers, and Other Dwellers of Imaginary Realms*. Guilford, CT: Lyons, 2009.

Sheila C. Murphy, *How Television Invented New Media*. Piscataway, NJ: Rutgers University Press, 2011.

Kevin Robert, *Cyber Junkie: Escape the Gaming and Internet Trap*. Center City, MN: Hazelden, 2010.

Michael Strangelove, *Watching YouTube: Extraordinary Videos by Ordinary People*. Toronto: University of Toronto Press, 2010.

Periodicals

Kalyn Belsha, "Video Games Not Just for Dudes, Dude," *Beaumont (TX) Enterprise*, August 22, 2010.

Victor Godinez, "Movie Studios Ramp Up Lawsuits over Illegal Downloads with Help from Internet Providers," *Dallas Morning News*, May 30, 2010.

Ellen McGirt, Tina Dupuy, and Danielle Sacks, "I Want My Twitter TV!," *Fast Company*, December 2010–January 2011.

Shari Roan, "Are Virtual-Game Players More Depressed?," *Los Angeles Times*, February 16, 2009.

Brian Steinberg, "The Future of TV," *Advertising Age*, November 30, 2009.

Internet Sources

Family Safe Media, "Pornography Statistics," 1998–2011. www.family safemedia.com/pornography_statistics.html.

Dennis G. Jerz, "Colossal Cave Adventure," *Jerz's Literacy Weblog*, September 10, 2010. http://jerz.setonhill.edu/if/canon/Adventure.htm.

Official Google Blog, "The Future of Online Video," September 16, 2008. http://googleblog.blogspot.com/2008/09/future-of-online-video.html.

Websites

GamerWidow (www.gamerwidow.com). Established by Sherry Myrow of Toronto, Canada, the website serves as a support group for spouses whose husbands and wives are addicted to online gaming. Visitors can read blog entries by members, enter a chat room, and access news reports addressing the issue of Internet addiction.

Vimeo (vimeo.com). Unlike YouTube, which is open to virtually anybody who wants to upload video onto the Internet, Vimeo has set higher standards, reserving space for amateur filmmakers who are serious about their craft. Viewers can browse categories such as art, music, nature, and comedy.

Index

Note: Boldface page numbers indicate illustrations.

Picture Credits

Cover: Thinkstock/Photodisc

Maury Aaseng: 8

AP Images: 11, 19, 22, 31, 43, 49, 52, 58, 61, 65

© Toby Melville/Reuters/Corbis: 39

Photofest: 71

Reuters/Mario Anzuoni/Landov: 26

About the Author

Hal Marcovitz is a former newspaper reporter and columnist who has written more than 150 books for young readers. As a journalist, he was called on to provide stories for both print and online readers. He makes his home in Chalfont, Pennsylvania.